# Infidelity

## ELISSA GOUGH

**AVERY**
a member of Penguin Group (USA) Inc.

Cover Designer: Phaedra Mastrocola
In-House Editor: Marie Caratozzolo
Typesetter: Gary A. Rosenberg

a member of
Penguin Group (USA) Inc
375 Hudson Street
New York, NY 10014
www.penguin.com

**Library of Congress Cataloging-in-Publication Data**

Gough, Elissa
    Infidelity : your complete guide to awareness, prevention, intervention,
and recovery / Elissa Gough.
        p. cm.
    ISBN 1-58333-002-x
    1. Adultery—United States. 2. Marriage—United States. 3. Sex (Psychology)
I. Title.

HQ806 .G68 2000
306.73'6—dc21                                          99-045644

Copyright © 2000 by Elissa Gough

Printed in the United States of America

10   9   8   7   6   5   4

# Contents

This book is dedicated to each of the men
who have been in and out of my life.

They have taught me a great deal
about the passion and pain of loving,
and each one has played an active role
in shaping who I am.

Beginning with my dad, these men were catalysts
for most of my decisions and choices.

Without them, I would have no story to tell.

# Acknowledgments

This book, which took a great deal of courage to write, is based upon the experiences of my life and the lives of many others who have been touched (and sometimes crushed) by infidelity along the way. I feel blessed for having been given the opportunity to make this endeavor a reality, and would like to express my sincere appreciation to all of those who have helped me realize this dream.

The professionalism and expertise of a number of people at Avery Publishing Group were instrumental in the creation of this book, and to them I am eternally grateful. First of all, I must thank publisher Rudy Shur for believing in me and giving me the opportunity to share my story in the first place. For her work in helping shape and develop the book, I owe a great deal of gratitude to my editor, Marie Caratozzolo. Her guidance and dedication to this project went way beyond the call of duty. And for her outstanding job in designing such a beautiful cover, I must extend a heartfelt thank you to Phaedra Mastrocola. In this case, you really *can* judge a book by its cover!

On a more personal note, for their love and support throughout this project, I must acknowledge my lifetime family of friends. They have been with me as my story has unfolded and as it continues to unfold. I must thank Ran Mullins, graphic artist extraordinaire, for his talents as well as his incredible patience. This book could not have happened without you. Sincere gratitude goes to my "robot," Chris Shea, for both his amazing, superhuman typing skills, and also for sharing his thoughts and feelings with me. What a blessing you have been. I must also acknowledge Joe Jotkowitz for his genuine efforts and dedication to this project. And of course, my sincere and loving appreciation goes to Dergie, whose constant encouragement and unwavering devotion gave me the motivation I needed to turn my vision into a reality. Thank you for not being scared off by my story!

And finally, a very special thank you must go to the dozens of individuals who were willing to share their thoughts and experiences in the pages of this book. Your stories will surely help make a difference.

# A Word From
# the Author

Whether you have chosen this book for yourself or
for someone else, you have taken an essential step
in increasing your awareness and understanding
of infidelity. Everyone has his or her interpretation of what
an affair is all about. Somewhere in this book, you will find
yourself, no matter which stage of this phenomenon you
are in.

Infidelity is a topic that continues to be highly exploited,
controversial, and is discussed more and more each day in
this country and throughout the world. You wonder who is
doing it? Should I be doing it? *Why can't I stop doing it?*
Perhaps you are flirting with the idea of having an affair. On
the other hand, maybe a friend of yours or a family member
is in the throes of an affair or in the end stages of such a relationship. Regardless of your position, this book will encourage you to consider certain realities of unfaithful behavior—
realities that you may have chosen to ignore or may have
been unaware of until now.

Child and spousal abuse, alcoholism, drug addiction,
compulsive gambling, and other social ills have all taken
their turn standing center stage in the spotlight. Identified as

catastrophic problems, these issues have been brought into the open and often successfully "treated." They have given rise to associations, counseling specialists, treatment centers, hotlines, and support groups for those needing both immediate and long-term care. Walk into any bookstore and you will find entire sections devoted to these behaviors—shelves overflow with informative books ranging from causes and characteristics of the problem to self-help programs and recovery techniques. Corporations, government agencies, universities, and non-profit organizations typically offer treatment programs for their employees who are caught in the web of such addictions. The world realizes how pervasive and destructive these social problems can be to individuals and the people around them.

Why is it, then, that in spite of the fact that infidelity continues to soar, it remains an orphan social ill? Why isn't it treated with the same challenge and urgency as other social issues? Certainly the damage and pain it causes can be just as devastating and far-reaching. Infidelity continues to be an issue surrounded by a wall of silence, embarrassment, and shame.

In a nonjudgmental and compassionate way, I have written *Infidelity: Your Complete Guide to Awareness, Prevention, Intervention, and Recovery*. It is intended to help raise the public's consciousness of the realities of unfaithfulness by bringing the deep-rooted drama of affairs into the open. Through practical and workable strategies and solutions, I show readers how to break down the walls that surround infidelity. This allows individuals the comfort zone needed to gain the skills, courage, and strength to face themselves, their partners, their families, and friends—in other words, face reality.

You may wonder why I consider myself, a former educator and nurse, such an expert on this subject. After all, I am not a psychologist, a medical doctor, or a member of the clergy. The answer is simple—through the course of my life, I have seen and done it all. I have been the betrayed spouse, the unfaithful wife, and the "other" woman. On all levels and from all aspects, I can identify with the passion, the pain, the elation, as well as the suffering that is caused by affairs. Nothing shocks or surprises me. I know firsthand the life cycle of an affair—how it is born, what gives it life, and how it inevitably ends. I am aware of the destruction an affair leaves in its wake. Having lived through numerous relationships, I understand all aspects of the triangle as well as the feelings and motivations of all those involved. Using these experiences as a foundation, I have written this book to share my knowledge. In turn, I hope you share this information with others.

For years I have helped guide individuals—no matter what their role—into learning more about the realities of adulterous behavior so they are better able to make informed choices. I have spent hundreds of hours conducting interviews, taking surveys, and facilitating support groups for the "other" man or woman, the betrayed partner, and the cheating party. I have also worked with children, parents, friends, next door neighbors, and extended family members whose lives have been touched in some way by infidelity.

Some people are determined to remain in their affairs, no matter what the risks or inevitable ramifications. I try to help these people see more clearly the consequences of their actions. For others who are looking for a way to end their affairs, together we develop workable strategies to help them achieve their goals. For those who want to recommit to their marriage or long-term relationship but find it difficult to forgive their unfaithful partners, we consider possible approaches they can take to save their relationships as well as their pride.

Today, I continue coaching people who have been directly involved or touched in some way by infidelity. As a team we work together to pick up the pieces of their lives, while examining options in order to move forward in positive directions.

While I do not condone infidelity, I do understand how and why it occurs. I realize its impact and know why affairs continue to thrive. My mission in writing this book is not to judge, moralize, or analyze, but to concentrate on the human aspects of betrayal and the attitudes and skills needed to begin to heal and recover from it. *Everyone should have the chance to change and the right to recovery.*

*Elissa Gough*

Elissa Gough

# Introduction

Christine and Bill worked in the same advertising agency. Both in their late thirties, they had an easy camaraderie and worked well together. About a year ago, they planned to share a cab after work to attend an annual gala sponsored by one of their largest accounts.

Before leaving the office, Bill caught himself admiring Christine, a slim brunette, as he watched her put on some lipstick and carefully undo the top button of her crisp white blouse. "You look sexy in that suit," he told her as they left for the party. She'd worn the suit, a severe black double-breasted light wool, quite often, but tonight she looked different, at least in Bill's eyes. More radiant somehow. The consummate businesswoman, Christine knew from her reading of upscale women's magazines just how to make the look work. Add a simple string of pearls and some frosted lipstick, unbutton the top button of your blouse, and, presto, you're ready for the most glamorous of functions.

The difference that night was that Christine really did feel sexy in a way she hadn't felt for a long time. She looked forward to going out. She had always been fond of Bill, they worked well together—and he looked extra handsome in his dark gray suit and funky tie. She felt a thrill when his hand accidentally touched hers as they waited for the elevator. The air between them seemed "charged" somehow.

At the party, they mingled with the crowd, networking with potential new clients, chatting with the people they knew. The food and wine were wonderful, and Bill and Christine enjoyed the evening immensely. Every so often their eyes met across the room, and once or twice they shared a private smile.

As the party drew to a close, Bill suggested they head back to the office for a minute to debrief before heading home to their respective spouses. Christine knew her husband was away on one of his usual business trips, so why not? She figured that it was already late, another hour wouldn't matter.

Back in Bill's roomy corner office, she kicked off her shoes and sat in what she knew was a provocative pose—legs up around the arm of the chair. When Bill handed Christine a glass of wine, they stared at each other for a moment, and then he suddenly leaned down and kissed her. She found herself responding.

Moments later, they were making love with a passion that shocked them both. Neither one knew just how it happened, but it was pure magic. Afterwards, Bill apologized, "I'm sorry. I don't know what came over me. You just looked so wonderful, and the evening went so well . . . and the clients love you . . . and you're just such a terrific . . . . Look, I know you're married and so am I . . . and I do love my wife, but she's so involved with the kids and . . . it just seems as though we haven't really communicated in any real way for years . . ."

Christine stopped Bill, "I'm not sorry." How could something that felt so right be wrong? "Sometimes you just have to follow your heart." Christine and her husband had been drifting apart for some time now. Each of them worked long hours. They had no children. She was sure that Bill was in a similar place emotionally.

Over the next few months, Bill and Christine took every

*opportunity possible to be together. They tried to be discreet, but it wasn't long before their colleagues guessed something was going on. Body language, proximity, and personal space change when two people are in love. And Christine and Bill were in love. They sent each other coded e-mail messages over the office system and met secretly as often as they could.*

*Then Bill's wife found out, and all hell broke loose . . .*

Infidelity is as old as history—and just as complicated. The mere fact that one of the Ten Commandments exhorts us against adultery is a sure sign that even in Biblical times people strayed. Today, high-profile examples of adultery are everywhere, from the front pages of newspapers to the back rooms of corporate offices. The evidence is all around us. The reality is that wherever there are relationships, there will also be betrayals.

Understanding why affairs happen is not as well understood. Answers, solutions, and explanations are buried deep inside glib analyses and psychological jargon that do little or nothing to help the people who are actually caught in the web of a love triangle. Even though we're fascinated by infidelity—we avidly read about in newspapers and watch it on soap operas—it seems as though we need to distance ourselves from any real exposure to this delicate subject. We love the juicy details, but we don't want to know how or why infidelity happens. We don't want to think about how easily it could happen to any of us.

Nor do we want to take an honest look at the damage infidelity can create, particularly to those least able to understand it—like our children. These deeper, human issues surrounding the ramifications of adultery rarely get discussed. A veil of secrecy continues to surround the subject—much the same way it once covered up other social problems like alcoholism and spousal abuse.

Part of the problem lies in the intensely human drama that surrounds infidelity. Love, attraction, passion, and commitment are not concepts we are able to analyze very well, even though psychology and the "science" of human behavior is over a hundred years old. Typically, our thoughts on adultery are mired in social norms and taboos. Perhaps that's why we find it easier simply to say "don't do it," rather than examine and deal with the motivations behind such behavior.

Whether you're the betrayed spouse or the one doing the betraying; whether you've initiated an affair or have given into one; whether you're the one clamoring for change inside your relationship or the one who wants everything to remain the same, you share with others in your situation a powerful array of emotions, of conflicted desires, of buried pain.

*Infidelity* provides answers and insights for anyone caught in a love triangle. It is not meant to replace professional help or be the final word on affairs. It is, however, different from any other book on the subject because it addresses age-old questions about betrayal, as well as the reasons and feelings behind such behavior. Using experiences and stories from real people—and sharing their solutions—this book deals with everyone in and around the triangle, even those who are only peripherally involved. It addresses such topics as: How and why do affairs begin? How do they develop? How do you end an affair and recover from its effects? Who gains from infidelity? Who loses?

Finally, this book shows the route to recovery and healing. It encourages you to look ahead to the consequences of affairs in order to understand and, therefore, prevent them. It covers the impact of infidelity on children and extended family members, as well as friends, acquaintances, and colleagues. It presents coping techniques for everyone affected—the betrayed party, the cheating partner, or the "other" man or woman.

This is not a book about judgments or moralizations, nor is it a book of rules. Rather, it is a book whose mission is to convey the reality of infidelity. It is a gamble, and even though you may think you're ahead, the odds of losing everything are stacked against you.

# PART ONE

# The Basics
# of
# Betrayal

# 1 Life Cycle of an Affair

*"Results are what you expect; consequences are what you get."*

—Anonymous

The life cycle of an affair is really quite simple (and far less complicated than the relationship itself). Every affair has three basic components—a birth, a life, and a death. Once born, it evolves into a shared journey, one that gives it life and enables it to take on unique characteristics and a personality of its own. Whether an affair lasts for one day or ten years, it will inevitably end. Its death can be caused by a mutual breakup or an angry parting of the ways. And even in those cases in which the participants marry, the act of marriage in and of itself signifies the death of the affair.

## WHAT IS AN AFFAIR?

One dictionary definition of an affair is "a romantic and sexual relationship, sometimes one of brief duration, between two people who are not married to each other." Another dictionary describes it as, "an amorous relationship between two people; an amour," while yet another source defines it as "an affaire de coeur" (an affair of the heart). To me, an affair is an illicit liaison verging on the scandalous or notorious. It is a betrayal; a relationship between two people who should not be having one, at least according to the acceptable norms of our society. It's a breach of trust that is further compounded by deceit.

Marriage, by contrast, implies safety and trust—a healthy connection of oneness in which you feel you know virtually everything there is to know about the other person. The basis for any marriage or long-term relationship is exclusivity. It's about two people with a bond so strong that they've made a public and private commitment to each other, a vow to stay together through thick and thin. We refer to a spouse or mate in the possessive—my husband, my wife, my partner. People in committed relationships share their day-to-day lives and innermost secrets. Ideally, they are bonded to each other emotionally, physically, and intimately. Everything surrounding this type of relationship, from the social and cultural concept of love to the phrasing of the wedding vows, is a clear demonstration that this bond is not to be shared. It is this "exclusion of others" that keeps the relationship safe and secure. Engaging in an affair breaches this exclusivity. It allows an intruder to break this bond.

The reality of affairs is often lost in the midst of the romanticism with which they are surrounded. The definitions mentioned earlier give affairs—which are essentially a breach of trust—an exciting spin. More realistically, an affair is a violation of a commitment that is further complicated and nurtured by ongoing secrets and lies. In fact, secrecy is one important element that makes an affair so seductive, appealing, and often so very dangerous. It gives affairs their spice, thrill, and sustenance. It becomes their lifeblood. Without secrecy, an illicit relationship is no longer illicit. Yet from the time we are children, we find ourselves drawn to secrets and hidden treasures, which are often wonderful sources of pleasure. Of course, affairs are rarely kept secret for long. In time, as the need for alibis and excuses become necessary, and as one or both parties become more reckless, the affair becomes more difficult to hide. The reality is, the life of an affair consists of a great deal of lies, some sex, and the playing out of one's fantasies.

In contrast to the almost thrilling definition of affair, the definition of *infidelity* is much less romantic. A typical dictionary definition decribes infidelity as, "unfaithfulness to a sexual partner, especially a spouse; an act of sexual unfaithfulness." Even more legal sounding, *adultery* is typically defined as "voluntary sexual intercourse between a married person and a partner other than the lawful spouse." These are stark reminders that the reality of an affair is far different from its idyllic definitions. Affairs are about deception, unfaithfulness, and lies; they are about letting down the person you have committed to love exclusively.

Yet infidelity seems to be all around us, from the bedrooms of the rich and famous to the boardrooms and offices of those in power. Nobody seems immune, not presidents nor princes nor people like you and me. Affairs are blind to race, religion, education, sexual orientation, and socio-economic status. Every once in a while, a high-profile incident hits the front pages and infidelity receives a brief flurry of attention, but essentially this subject is dealt with as though it is not really a problem but a fact of life. The entertainment industry certainly doesn't help. Soap operas and films and novels make it sound as though cheating on one's spouse must be okay since so many people are doing it.

## "HAPPILY EVER AFTER"

Perhaps one of the most destructive myths we've been taught (especially during our younger, more impressionable years) is the "happily ever after" fairy tale ending. This theme's underlying message, which continues to be re-enacted in plays and movies and books, is that conflicts are resolved by the time a commitment is made. The prince and princess inevitably manage to break the evil spell or conquer the wicked villain so they can find one another and happily ride off into the sunset. The music swells, the credits roll, and that's the end of the story. Everything works out, and the main characters live happily ever after.

What makes a good story, however, does not necessarily bear much resemblance to everyday life. Real life rarely has neat solutions and happily-ever-after endings. It just doesn't happen. I certainly have not met anyone who's started his or her life's journey with a path as clearly set as the ones found in fairy tales or in the movies—find the magic goblet, claim your kingdom, and save the good guys. In fiction, there is that magical genie or fairy godmother who pops up at just the right moment with a handy spell or two. In movies, there's that special someone on the "inside" who gives the hero just the right advice and just in the nick of time. Even sit-coms manage to have a friend or two to help out with the perfect solution to a problem before the half hour is up. Quite the contrary when it comes to the realities of everyday living.

Real life is perplexing, involved, and often hurtful. Rarely are its problems cleanly or easily resolved. Unlike what we see in movies or sitcoms, real life carries its price tags, regrets, and hard-learned lessons. And by chance, if we do fall in love and get married, it isn't the end of the tale but the beginning. The passion, the excitement, and the thrilling ups and downs we experience when dating do not paint an accurate picture of what married life is necessarily going to be like. These "electrically charged" feelings are a part of the process two people experience when getting to know each other.

The day-to-day reality of waking up every morning to the same person is simply not a factor in fiction. Neither is the extent to which real life can get tiresome or just plain boring. The reasons are obvious—actual day-to-day living just does not hold the right kind of dramatic flair that makes for an exciting story. So, the excitement and drama we see on soap operas and in the movies do not prepare us for reality. The truth is that life doesn't read like a novel. Things often *aren't* very thrilling or exciting on a day-to-day basis. The daily grind *can* get mundane. Yes, life *can* become a bit humdrum.

When I was in my early twenties, certainly nobody had prepared me for the sudden letdown of my first marriage after all the fuss and excitement of being in love, getting engaged, and having a lavish wedding. I expected my marriage to be nothing short of the fairy tales I had eagerly listened to as a child. This marriage, which lasted less than a year, took place when I was in college and still reeling from the shock of my father's tragic and unexpected death from a heart attack. His sudden loss instantly removed the foundation upon which my life had drawn its strength and security. The nucleus of my family had changed drastically, and I was left feeling alone and frightened. My fear of abandonment was further reinforced by my mother's ongoing mental illness. So when the law student I had been dating asked me to marry him, I accepted, believing that marriage would be a source of security—an assurance that I wouldn't be left alone any longer.

Like many women of my generation, I was convinced that falling in love and getting married paved the road to happiness. Today, I realize the extent to which I had been influenced by those movies with the perfect endings, the romantic stories, the fairy tales. Almost immediately after we had taken our wedding vows, I realized that I'd made a terrible mistake. I had gotten married partially out of fear of being alone and partially out of gratitude for the compassion my new husband had shown me during my time of need. Several weeks later, wedding presents were returned and my marriage ended in an annulment. I simply apologized to those who had been affected by the breakup. I was not ready to take more responsibility than that for my actions. I continued to hide from my pain by returning to school where I completed my undergraduate studies in elementary education. It kept me feeling somewhat safe from the world.

This experience was a short but significant chapter in my life. It clearly demonstrated how I had expected marriage to be the answer for my insecurities and the pain I was feeling. I thought it would provide that happy ending I so desperately needed.

## COMMITMENT DOES NOT END TEMPTATION

In the book of Genesis, when Eve takes a bite of the apple, the "forbidden fruit," she is actually committing a form of emotional adultery. By listening to the voice of evil, she is unfaithful to her covenant with God, creating the notion of original sin—an essential and pivotal concept in the human condition. It doesn't matter whether or not we believe in the biblical notions of sin and betrayal, the real issue is that most of us, at some point in our lives, will be tempted by someone or something that is not in our best interest.

When people first fall in love and get married, most become oblivious to the outside world and its inherent temptations. They have found the person they feel is their destiny, the one with whom they are ready to live out their lives. Typically, new lovers find themselves with stars in their eyes and magic in their hearts. During this time, rarely, if ever, do they find themselves attracted to others—the focus of their love occupies their thoughts and desires exclusively. They believe that this state of bliss will endure without change throughout the years. "I couldn't even think of looking at another man (or woman)," is the way most people feel when they first fall in love or are just beginning a life together. The search is over. Simply being married or in a committed relationship, however, doesn't guarantee that somewhere down the road you will not be tempted or fall in love with someone other than your partner. We like to believe that the person we commit to is the only one that destiny has chosen for us. In reality, however, there are many individuals with whom we could find love.

Marriage vows or the commitment to a relationship do not shut down the physiological and psychological process we call attraction. It's human nature to seek new experiences, to be curious, to enjoy many things, and be drawn to many people. And there's nothing inherently wrong with feeling attracted to someone else. After all, we live in a world in which every day someone somewhere is trying to lure us into *something*—buying things we can't afford, eating luscious foods that lack nutrition, playing hooky from work to spend a day at the beach. We wouldn't be human if we didn't find ourselves drawn to things that we shouldn't be now and then. And it's not uncommon for those in a committed relationship to be attracted to people other than their partners. This intrigue could be for a coworker, someone we meet at the gym, a new business client, or even a person we find ourselves chatting with while standing in line at the supermarket or bank.

The issue is not whether we experience feelings of attraction now and then, but what we do with these emotions. Countless men and women remain faithful to their partners despite the occasional flirtations or infatuations they may feel for someone else. They just don't act on their fantasies. Silver and golden wedding anniversaries celebrating faithful relationships still exist. Even former President and devout Baptist Jimmy Carter admitted that he had "looked on a lot of women with lust" and "committed adultery" in his heart. But he never acted on these attractions. He had the conviction to resist temptation, and his fantasies remained just that—fantasies.

So what makes some people play out their fantasies while others resist their impulses? Why is it that some people in seemingly good marriages can't resist giving into the temptation to stray, while others who feel trapped in unhappy marriages cannot bring themselves to participate in an extramarital affair? The answer lies in respect for themselves and for their partners. Some people take their commitments more seriously than others regardless of the hurdles they encounter. On the other hand, many people find themselves questioning their relationships at the first sign of a problem or temptation. When the fairy tale hasn't worked out as had been expected, they believe they are living the wrong story line. They aren't living "happily ever after," and for this they may blame their partners. They believe that their soul mate is still out there somewhere. Infidelity is sometimes a defiant response to this disillusioned fantasy, as they search for that ideal mate. Many individuals may decide to write off their relationships because it is less appealing and more difficult work through the hard times. At the onset of betrayal, affairs often become that fairy tale people are searching for.

## HOW MY FAIRY TALE REALLY ENDED

Reflecting back, when I didn't like the story line of my life, I created a new one. I became the epitome of what affairs are all about. Following the completion of my undergraduate work in elementary education at the University of Cincinnati in Ohio, I visited some friends in Southern California. It was a visit that was to continue for most of my adult life. In the early 1960s, California was a place of invention, a land of sunshine and opportunity. I discarded the old rules I had lived by in the Midwest and felt free to invent new ones. Dorothy's journey to the Land of Oz could not have been more amazing than my journey from staid and proper Cincinnati to the flash and glamour of Beverly Hills.

One day, my friends insisted I see the desert community of Palm Springs. It was there, at a popular resort, that I met a man who would soon become my husband and the father of my only child. After a brief whirlwind courtship, we decided to elope. We honeymooned briefly in Mexico, then settled happily in the austere beauty and agreeable desert climate of Palm Springs. I was mesmerized by my surroundings. Everything—the physical beauty of the desert, the sunlight, the flowers, and the sunsets, as well as the immense and reckless wealth of some of the people who lived there—enchanted me. With my teaching degree, I found a position in a private school, where I taught until our daughter was born.

I put my teaching career on hold to become a full-time mom. It was the most joyful of times. I believed I finally had it all—a loving husband, a beautiful child whom we adored, and a home in the most idyllic of locations. But a year later, without any warning, my fairy tale life came to an abrupt halt and was replaced by every parent's worst nightmare. Our fragile young child was diagnosed with acute lymphopsytic leukemia, a dreadful systemic cancer with a very poor prognosis, especially at that time. The doctors gave her six months to live.

Suddenly, my husband and I found ourselves caught up in a blur of long days and sleepless nights. We literally lived in hospitals as our daughter underwent an endless stream of blood transfusions, tests, and treatments. We were haunted by the pressing feeling of helplessness. I read everything I could get my hands on, hoping against hope that someone, somewhere, had discovered something that could cure her. I fully expected that my knowledge would somehow be able to save her. This led to my decision to enroll in nursing school.

Over the next several years, my husband and I searched and prayed for that one miracle, that scientific breakthrough, anything that would save our child and spare her pain and suffering. We hung on to any small glimmer of hope in order to get us through each day. Gradually, the strain began to affect our relationship. Together, we continued to love and care for our daughter, but somehow the bond between us began to dissolve in the whirlpool of suffering that constantly surrounded us. I began to withdraw from my husband, who dealt with his agony by immersing himself in a new career. I totally lost sight of the fact that I needed to nurture and care for him as well as our daughter. Since I wasn't able to find any peace and comfort for myself, I had no strength to help him through his grief. The more lost and grief-stricken I felt over our daughter, the more distant my relationship with my husband became, and our marriage continued to fall apart.

My first extramarital affair occurred during this time. The relationship was with one of my daughter's doctors, a man who had shown concern and compassion for our child throughout her illness. At the time, I had no idea why I entered the affair. I had never been unfaithful in a relationship before, nor was sex the reason. Looking back, I believe my involvement was driven by the urgency to fulfill a fantasy that I desperately needed at that time—that this physician, with his expertise and genuine caring, would be the key to our child's survival, that he could somehow save her. After a five-year struggle, however, my daughter lost her battle.

What followed next was a period fraught with such intense grief, sadness, guilt, and shame that my coping abilities were drained. I wanted only to run away, to block the reminders of my past. These empty feelings became responsible for several poor choices and unwise decisions that would affect me for years to come. I bitterly regretted having had the brief affair and felt that my husband deserved more than an unfaithful wife. I believed that I couldn't erase the dark shadow of my betrayal from our marriage. So with my daughter gone and a heart filled with pain and remorse, I divorced my husband and tried to escape my grief with a new beginning. Once again, the destruction of my family's nucleus had left me feeling alone and abandoned.

Soon after, I left California and returned to Cincinnati to hide again, this time in graduate school. At the time, it seemed like an appropriate bandage, but in retrospect, I realize what I needed most was to face my grief, not run from it. My behavior, I have since come to realize, set into motion a pattern that would surface again and again in the years to come. For rather than confronting my daughter's death and working through the consequences of my affair with my husband—who was the only person truly capable of sharing my grief—I decided to run away, erase the past along with anyone and anything that reminded me of the heart-wrenching experience I had just lived through. I had to start over. But we can never undo the past. We cannot deny what has already happened. Before we can begin to heal, we must be courageous enough to face our hurt and connect with our past, not run from it. It took over thirty years for me to realize that no matter how hard we try to run away from grief, it will be there waiting for us, if and when we decide to face it.

Reflecting back, the way I dealt with my grief and suffering, for the most part, was unthinking and naïve. For a time, I shut everyone out, including professionals, and tried to find solutions for myself, except that my solutions only created more problems in the long run. Unfortunately, at that time I was reacting to the hand life had dealt me. Few people, thankfully, will have to go through the same tragic circumstances I did. Like me, however, most people will, at some time or another, feel the need to detach themselves from a different untenable or difficult situation.

## TESTING LOVE

My first affair illustrates in highly dramatic fashion the extent to which the fantasies we've built around marriage and commitment can impede our ability to handle the many significant issues that confront us. For an affair is merely a continuation of the fantasy. In my case, it illustrates the road I chose to avoid facing the painful, heartfelt issues I needed to come to terms with.

Falling in love is, in its own way, a magnificent obsession. For some, though, it is a way of ignoring or sidestepping reality to avoid dealing with various problems. I believed I was in love with my child's doctor, and that love insulated me from the pain of having to deal with my daughter's illness. The affair created a false sense of security for me. Love also shields us from other unpleasant or monotonous aspects of life, such as working long hours, dealing with small children, cooking meals, or doing laundry. Love also gives us the strength to cope with more serious challenges, such as unemployment, illness, a disabling accident, or death of a loved one.

According to Dr. Frank Pittman, M.D., author of *Private Lies: Infidelity and the Betrayal of Intimacy* (New York: W.W. Norton & Co., 1990), the "in love" state is an obsession that is based more on fantasy than reality. People often look for love to ease the stressful realities of their lives, and this search is often the catalyst that propels people into affairs. Dealing with death or illness of a loved one, raising children, facing an "empty nest," or living with a disinterested spouse are some common reasons that cause people to look for the soothing balm of love. From years of facilitating and participating in support groups relating to infidelity, I must agree with Dr. Pittman—people often engage in affairs to feel the love that helps them evade and avoid the sometimes painful realities of their lives.

## SUMMING IT UP

In our society, love and marriage have become romantic ideals. Many people honestly believe that true love causes everything to fall into place and run smoothly. And when it doesn't, they assume what they are experiencing isn't true love, and they must search for it elsewhere—often through an affair. In the next chapter, you will see how unrealistic expectations and everyday problems can easily lead to infidelity and betrayal.

# 2 | Beyond Flirtation

*"Men are always doomed to be duped, not so much by the arts of the [female] sex as by their own imaginations. They are always wooing goddesses and marrying mere mortals."*

—Washington Irving, 1822

*A*fter Carol's boyfriend ended their difficult three-year relationship, she was feeling a bit bruised. Trying to keep herself busy, she became actively involved in her church, where she met Mike. The gossip around the church was that Mike and his wife didn't get along very well and were headed for divorce.

While advocating changes in church policies and administration, Carol and Mike found themselves working together a lot. They enjoyed each other's company, and sometimes after a meeting they would go for a cup of coffee at a nearby café. Mike listened to Carol's stories about her ex-boyfriend and sympathized with her recent breakup. Carol seemed genuinely interested in any topic Mike brought up. She laughed at his jokes and made him feel important. Soon, they found themselves growing more and more attracted to each other, and their occasional coffee dates began to occur more regularly. After a few weeks, they found themselves in bed together.

When Mike's wife left for a vacation, which was really a

*trial separation, the affair between Mike and Carol intensi-*
*fied. The couple soon became careless about the privacy of*
*their meetings, and people began spotting them together. By*
*the time Mike's wife returned, he felt guilt-ridden and*
*decided to try and reconcile with her. Unfortunately, the*
*news of Mike and Carol's liaison had reached the ears of*
*Mike's wife, as well as several members of the church com-*
*munity. Mike lost face with the church board in spite of his*
*attempts at reconciling with his wife. To this day, Mike and*
*his wife struggle to keep their marriage intact, while Carol*
*moved on in search of that fairy tale ending.*

As you can see from this story, affairs are often sparked by
two people who are hungry for communication, for contact.
The relationship they have with their partners may lack the
warmth and sensitivity they need. When someone new suddenly appears and seems attentive, there may be hours of talking, chattering, bantering, flirting, and listening. Of course,
the primary reason for this wave of interest is that the new
person is a stranger—someone who doesn't know anything
about us—who we are, where we went to school, or the details of our childhood. This individual is unaware of how we
feel about our work or the books we read or the TV shows
we enjoy. Nor does he or she know our favorite color, how
we handle anger and disappointment, or what we look like
first thing in the morning. A relationship with someone new
gives us a chance to reinvent ourselves—to put our best foot
forward.

Certainly you went through this "getting-to-know-you"
process with your spouse or partner at some point early in
your relationship. Remember? It helped you decide to get together in the first place and continue to nurture the relationship. After a few years of living together, however, you may
have begun to feel that you knew everything there was to
know about your partner, and that your partner knew you too
well (or not well enough in some cases). Suddenly, a new person appears who is interested in hearing everything about you.

Sometimes, in long-term relationships couples no longer *really* talk to or listen to one another. They tune each other out. Conversation becomes limited to issues regarding children, the home, finances, and everyday happenings at work. Linguist Deborah Tannen, Ph.D., in *You Just Don't Understand*, discusses the different communication styles of men and women. She maintains that much of the silence between couples results from the lack of understanding each partner has for the other's "conversational style." Women, Tannen feels, generally talk to create closeness and intimacy. They've been brought up to associate friendship and closeness with communication of feelings, desires, relationships, and other ambiguous details. Men, on the other hand, typically associate talking with information and problem solving. Take that famous cartoon in which the man is buried behind the newspaper while his wife is seething at his lack of interest in what she is saying. The problem between them lies in the way each one assesses the situation. The man feels as if he has nothing to say at that point; he simply wants to eat his meal and enjoy his paper. The woman interprets his silence as disinterest and a general failure to communicate.

"For everyone, home is a place to be offstage," writes Tannen. But the peace and solace of home are open to different interpretations for women and men. To men, home often represents comfort, a place where they can just be themselves and not feel the pressure to prove themselves to anyone. They don't feel the need to talk. Women, on the other hand, generally feel that home represents a place where they can talk freely and express every feeling and emotion. They tend to talk constantly to those closest to them. Home is a comfort zone in which they can be themselves without fear of ridicule.

Of course, these generalizations certainly don't apply to all couples, but they are indications of the differences in men and women. Complacency and lack of communication within a marriage or serious relationship can foster an environment in which infidelity can flourish. Withdrawal on the part of either person, regardless of the reason, can easily result in one or both partners feeling that their needs are being ignored, misunderstood, or denigrated. So when temptation strikes in the form of infidelity, it suddenly becomes a lot easier to pay attention to and possibly give into it.

## TYPES OF AFFAIRS

There are a variety of categories into which most affairs fall. The following list presents the most common types of affairs, many of which exhibit characteristics that may cross over into a number of different categories.

❏ *Love affair.* Feelings of love are present in this type of affair, but the married or committed party does not want to break up his or her marriage.

❏ *Non-committal affair.* An affair in which very little, if any, personal, intimate information is shared. The rules, which involve no mention of spouses or partners, are established up front. Committed parties have no intention of leaving their partners.

❏ *Perk affair.* An affair in which money, gifts, and other material items are given by one party in exchange for fulfillment of desires. Gigolos and "kept" mistresses fall into this category.

❏ *Quickie affair.* An affair characterized by an unwillingness of the participants to give much of their time or money. One-night stands are an example of this type of affair.

❏ *Sex-only affair.* An affair based primarily on sex. Feelings of love and/or caring are not part of this type of relationship, which is usually short-lived.

❏ *"Wake-up-call" affair.* In this type of affair, the goal of at least one party is actually to get caught. He or she uses infidelity as a means of alerting his or her partner that something is wrong in the relationship.

❏ *Long-term affair.* As its name implies, this is an affair that has been going on for an extended period of time—often years. In some cases, the betrayed partner is totally oblivious to the affair; in other cases, he or she may be aware of the affair's existence but willing to turn a blind eye to it.

❏ *Secret affair.* While all affairs are secretive to some degree, in this type of affair, it is the secret itself that gives the relationship its passion and excitement. Once this affair has been discovered and the secret is out, the relationship usually fizzles.

❏ *Open affair.* An affair in which the betrayed partner is fully aware of the infidelity of his or her mate. In many cultures, such as affair is viewed as a symbol of status and power.

❏ *Thrill-of-the-chase affair.* An affair born of a flirtatious, manipulative chase. This relationship often ends shortly after the conquest.

❏ *Cyber affair.* An affair that takes place over the Internet. The thrill of a secret rendezvous with a stranger is what gives this relationship its appeal. (See "Love on the Internet" on page 24.)

Yes, affairs fall into a variety of categories. But why are affairs born in the first place? As you will see, the reasons can be just as varied.

## WHY PEOPLE HAVE AFFAIRS

Although the reasons for having affairs are as numerous and individual as the people who have them, most fall into some very basic categories. Loneliness, the need for attention, sexual satisfaction, and the desire for romance are just a few of the common causes. Let's take a closer look at some of the most typical reasons people cheat.

# Love on the Internet

*After the workplace, the Internet is the most common site for people to "meet." With more and more people navigating online, there has been a dramatic increase in the number of cyber affairs—flings that provide the thrill of an extramarital rendezvous between strangers. These affairs, which typically originate in online chat rooms, involve people who are free to reinvent themselves and take on new and exciting roles with the people they meet. Remaining anonymous, they are able to create a romantic illusion.*

*Why are people drawn to chat rooms in the first place? Many admit their initial reason is curiosity, while others claim they are motivated by boredom. The initial connection with another person often begins with an innocent online chat in which the two parties discover they have a lot in common with each other. This Internet interplay often leads the parties into a real online obsession. Never having seen or touched each other, they share passionate intimacies through electronic communication. Viewing their online loves as soul mates, a number of people have actually left their partners as a result.*

*Most interesting, these affairs do not involve physical contact. Instead, they gain their strength from shared emotional intimacies and sexual fantasies. This sharing, which may start out innocently, can escalate into a romantic interlude that is so strong, it becomes more important than the marriage itself. A betrayed partner typically views a cyber affair as a breach of trust. Many couples are unable to reconcile after such a discovery and the marriage falls apart.*

## Loneliness

Loneliness—both emotionally and physically—can prove devastating to a relationship. A spouse or partner who feels emotionally abandoned or alone is an easy target for temptation—and infidelity. An affair may seem like a way to ease the pain and erase feelings of solitude and loneliness. By the same token, those individuals whose partners are physically withdrawn or away from the home a great deal for whatever reason—business, social activities, hobbies—may be drawn to someone else for companionship and validation.

Of course, anyone can feel lonely from time to time, but a constant state of loneliness signifies trouble. The man who sits alone in front of the television set every day, warming up his meals in the microwave while his wife is out playing bridge or surfing the Internet chat rooms may feel such isolation. These feelings also may be felt by the woman who spends most of her time managing the household and overseeing the activities of her children with little physical or emotional support from her husband. Basically, loneliness can be felt by anyone who feels that he or she is living a "single" life within the relationship.

Loneliness can make one vulnerable to the kindness and caring of others. A simple display of interest from someone new can spark a friendship that can deepen into something more than what was anticipated at the onset.

## Need for Attention

Lack of attention is easily translated into lack of caring and concern. Such feelings can work themselves into an affair. If a person in a relationship feels ignored, deprived, or lacking any kind of real attention from his or her partner—affection, loving gestures, conversation, general kindness—that person may feel compelled to search for that attention from someone else.

A wife whose husband would rather turn to the newspaper or watch television when she tries to tell him about her day may feel this lack of attention. A husband whose wife is constantly on the telephone, or always seems to be more interested in the children or in her own activities than in his interests, may experience the same shunned feeling. Additionally, it's important to feel recognized and cared for when we aren't feeling well, when we're weighed down by stress, or any time we're feeling unhappy or preoccupied. One Canadian poll found that nearly a quarter of dog owners and a fifth of cat owners believe their pets pay more attention to them than their spouses do. That's pretty sad. It's no wonder that people end up in the arms of those who will listen, care for, and give them the attention and loyalty they seek.

## Need for Romance

When two people enter an affair because they have fallen madly and passionately in love, this becomes an affair of the heart (or, as the French say, *affaire de coeur*). This type of affair can be the most entangled and potentially the most destructive. Love is impossible to describe, although poets and scholars have attempted to for centuries. And while romantic love is the subject of many films and books, it is difficult to understand. Love is something we search for, strive to attain, run from, hide behind, and suffer from. From my own experience, I know that when two people fall romantically in love, it feels like pure magic. Nothing is more important than the feelings they have for each other. This type of affair becomes all consuming as the lovers eagerly anticipate the next time they will be together. Everything and everyone else pales in comparison. Usual responsibilities are neglected and are replaced with passionate daydreams of love and desire.

Romance brings a whole new dimension to one's life. It makes everything seem more alive, exciting, and colorful. A person involved in a romantic affair typically tends to view his or her lover as a soul mate, the one true match. If love occurred in a vacuum, as it does in fiction, this kind of love would be pure ecstasy; but when marriages and children are sucked into this deceitful vortex, the results are catastrophic, devastating. For me, the times I spent with my last lover were some of the most joyful and fulfilling days of my life. There was, however, a price to pay as our affair eventually destroyed my family and nearly ended his.

## Need for Friendship

Mutual respect, a deep and abiding friendship and enjoyment for each other's company through shared interests or activities can be enough to propel two people into an affair. What might begin as companionship can deepen to the point at which sexual intimacy may seem like the next logical step. The opposite, however, is usually the case. What attracts us to our friends is often very different from what draws us to lovers. Platonic friends sometimes fool themselves into believing they can handle an affair because of their former smooth relationship. The fact, however, is that friendships change dramatically when sexual intimacy is introduced.

Shared interests are sometimes enough of a catalyst to draw two people into an affair. This is a common occurrence in the workplace. The work environment is a haven for many types of people. Unlike the home, where chores, children, chaos, and neverending demands make up much of the day, the typical workplace has well-defined goals and boundaries. For both sexes, a colleague can seem very appealing. The close working ties that result from being thrown together for long periods of time, perhaps on projects of shared interest, may cause coworkers to feel closer to each other intellectually and emotionally than they do with their partners waiting at home.

## Sexual Desire

Engaging in one-night stands, consorting with someone from an escort service, or seeking out prostitutes are behaviors that fall into the "pure sexual desire" category. Affairs in which two people meet purely out of lust and a desire to have sex are very rare. Of course it's not uncommon for consenting adults to want to have sex with someone who is not their partner, but to enter into an affair purely for sex is not common. Those who are looking to simply satisfy their sexual cravings generally don't want the complicated emotional ties and entanglements that affairs usually bring.

Although these types of affairs are uncommon, generally speaking, men are more likely to be drawn to them than women. Women usually crave emotional intimacy first.

## Sexual Addiction

The profile of sexual addicts is simple—they are driven to satisfy pure lust. Their need for sex is so important, it often causes them to deny the apparent risks they take from engaging in such affairs. Both men and women have risked fame, fortune, and precious relationships because they could not and would not control their philandering behavior. A sexual addict may have affairs simply for the sake of sexual satisfaction, not because there is any real "reason" to betray his or her partner. Some sex addicts are collectors of pornography, and may be drawn to group sex, masochism, and sadism.

Psychologists estimate that somewhere between 5 and 10 percent of Americans are sexual addicts. There are nearly a thousand branches of Sex and Love Addicts Anonymous in the United States. This twelve-step program is modeled after Alcoholics Anonymous (AA). Although once believed to be exclusively a male-dominated problem, sexual addiction is also on the rise in females as well.

There are many similarities between affairs based on sexual addiction and those born from sexual desire. The difference, however, lies in the emotions involved. Sex addicts often experience emotional ties while they are engaged in the sexual act. Those who are drawn into an affair purely for sexual desire tend to be more detached, less involved emotionally with their lovers.

## Desire for Power and Control

In some sense, all relationships are about power. The odds of a successful marriage increase as long as both parties agree on how the internal power structure of their relationship is formed and shared. It is only when something or someone changes, or one of the parties becomes dissatisfied with the structure of their partnership, that the struggle for power may cause the road to become bumpy. This increases the chances of having an affair.

There are many people in the world who are "controllers." They feel the need to be in charge, to feel a sense of power. They must hold the reins over their lives and generally over the lives of those around them, including their coworkers, children, friends, and partners. Individuals with controlling personalities tend to surround themselves with people who are "yes men"—those who are comfortable with and willing to be subservient, those who don't mind being controlled by another. Typically, when controllers fall in love, they pair themselves with partners who are willing to sublimate their own identities in order to keep peace; people who are willing to put aside their own wishes and desires to keep harmony in the relationship.

It is not unusual for controlling individuals to feel almost drunk with power, often on a subconscious level, and to assume that any actions they choose can be corrected by their own reactions. In relationships, their need to control emotions takes center stage, and they may enter into affairs to demonstrate this power. They choose who will love them and whom they will love. Decisions to start and/or end affairs become power plays in a test of wills.

But what about the dominated party in the relationship—the one who is controlled? It is not unusual for this partner, at some point, to break out from the control under which he or she lives. An affair may become a way to reassert his or her own identity and power. It could be a way of winning, a way of getting back at the person who seems to wield the power; a way of gaining back the sense of freedom and power that the partnership has robbed them of.

## Revenge

In many situations, revenge is the primary reason for entering into an affair. Most obviously, if one partner in the relationship has been unfaithful, the other partner may retaliate by carrying on an affair of his or her own. "You've had an affair, so now I will too."

People also have affairs to avenge hurtful situations and slights that have gone unnoticed or unresolved. For example, take the situation in which a husband accepts a job transfer and moves his family to a new place, a place where his wife feels isolated and alone. She may cheat on her husband as a form of rebellion. Or consider the wife who constantly mocks the physical appearance of her husband. He may have an affair to get back at his wife for her hurtful barbs and to prove (to both his wife and himself) that *somebody* thinks he's attractive.

Vengeful affairs can be sparked for any number of issues. For instance, one party may be sick and tired of the miserly nature of the other, or of his or her lack of involvement with the children. Reasons are diverse and to some may seem petty, but to the people involved, they are very real and provide justification for the affairs.

## A Potpourri of Reasons

In addition to the reasons just presented, there are a myriad of other motivations that cause people to have affairs. People don't have blueprints for what to do when a relationship doesn't seem to be working out. There are no definitive instruction booklets for ways to handle the natural strains and stresses of living with another person day in and day out.

For example, people who married at a very young age may suddenly feel that life has passed them by and may want to "experiment." For others, an affair may be cathartic—a "celebration" of a milestone in one's life. It may result as a means of amusement, or as a diversionary tactic for masking real issues or problems within the relationship. Some people have affairs because they want out of a marriage and can't think of any "nice" way to do it. Having an affair and getting caught simplifies the decision. An affair can be a means of boosting one's ego, or the result of a mid-life crisis or real-life tragedy such as the illness of a spouse. It can even be somewhat accidental or unplanned.

Whether it stems from feelings of loneliness within the marriage, a need for closeness and intimacy, or the result of falling in love with someone else, the decision to begin an affair has its roots in something deep within the participants themselves. It is something that prompts them to cut a symbolic ribbon and step across into the world of infidelity and betrayal.

## SHEDDING EVERYDAY ROLES

One of the most common reasons people cite for their unfaithfulness is the desire for variety, something new and different. A committed relationship carries with it roles and responsibilities, which can become constricting and confining, especially over time. An affair may seem like a way to break free. It allows, for instance, the woman who is drowning in her role as responsible wife and mother, to transform herself into an exciting femme fatale. An affair allows the man who feels restricted in his role as hard-working husband and father to take on the new role of Casanova.

In our society we've constructed various expectations around the role of wife, husband, mother, father, daughter-in-law, and all the other parts within a marriage or relationship. Often these roles duplicate those we witnessed as children. Without a second thought, we may replay the roles we saw our parents or perhaps our friends' parents playing—fathers mow lawns and play golf and mothers drive the kids to piano lessons. Other common roles include those of the chauffeur, the cook, and the breadwinner. There's the person who characteristically takes out the garbage, resolves the conflicts, takes charge of the finances, or carves the holiday turkey. Over time, these roles become well entrenched, and their restrictive natures may become at least part of the reason so many people feel the need to break free and search for new roles. A hidden relationship may seem like an ideal way for people to shed their roles and become simply "themselves." To them, an affair represents newness, a fresh start, thrills, and freedom without the onerous responsibilities that they've taken on in their everyday "real life" roles.

In an article that appeared in *Psychology Today*, Baltimore psychologist Shirley Glass agrees with the concept that affairs are often the result of a person desiring to break free of certain roles. "Affairs are often a chance for people to try out new behaviors, to dress in a different costume, to stretch and grow and assume a different role. In a long-term relationship, we often get frozen in our roles."

Ironically, the way in which many people behave in affairs would, in most cases, be precisely the shot in the arm that their marriages could use. Think about it for a moment. Someone who feels like a fixture in the home may begin a wild and passionate affair in which he or she is able to be sexually uninhibited. Suddenly this person feels sexy and attractive. Now envision this same kind of uninhibited behavior breathing new life into an existing relationship.

## SUMMING IT UP

Whether affairs stem from feelings of loneliness within the partnership, a need for closeness and intimacy, or the result of falling in love with someone else, the decision to begin an affair has its roots in something deep within the participants themselves. This is what prompts committed couples to cut through their exclusive bond and step into the world of fantasy and betrayal.

# PART TWO

# The
# Players

# 3 More Than a Three-Sided Triangle

*"Serving one's own passions is the greatest slavery."*

— Thomas Fuller, 1732

In geometric terms, a triangle is a simple three-sided figure. So when we speak about the "triangle" of an adulterous relationship, it's obvious who represents the three sides. They are the two primary players who are having the affair plus the third party—the one being betrayed. The reality, however, is that this triangle, unlike the one you've learned about in math class, has a lot more than three sides.

## THE CAST OF CHARACTERS

No matter which side of the triangle you're on, I can identify with you. I've lived each of the roles. I understand them. And from them I have learned valuable lessons. What I have also come to realize is that an affair is not just about the two primary players. When two people succumb to their initial attraction to each other and begin an affair, rarely, if ever, do they realize that they are putting their most treasured relationships on the line. To start with, there will be at least one betrayed spouse who will never regain the same trust he or she once had in the relationship—someone who will not regard the marriage in quite the same way again. Similarly, children, careers, and emotional and financial equity suffer, as does one's good name, friendships, family relationships, and social standings. And one more thing—once the cat is out of the bag, the relationship between you and your lover will change as well.

Three players may make up the main sides of a love triangle, but you can be sure that on the periphery lie a bewilderingly large number of people who will also be drawn in and involved in some way.

## The Principal Players

As discussed in Part One, the most active participants in extramarital affairs tend to be married people seeking to fulfill some need or expectation that their primary relationship lacks. The married person who enters an affair usually brings additional "baggage" inside the triangle that must be considered—perhaps children, financial assets, or social status. Rarely, if ever, is divorce part of the married "player's" plan. No matter how emotionally or financially draining, the marriage is usually expected to remain intact.

Many of those who occupy the second side of the triangle—the "lovers"—may even enter into a relationship, not realizing that the person they are involved with is married. However, once the affair is underway and they're hooked, spouse or no spouse, typically, they don't want to let go. Whether the lover is a mistress or the "other man," chances are this person will hang on to his or her lover at all costs. Characteristically, lovers tend to settle for a divided heart, continuous lies, broken promises, unmet dates and deadlines, and ongoing disappointments, as seen in the following story:

*I can't believe how naïve I was. How could I have fallen for all of the deception and lies that surrounded my four-year love affair with Richard? So much of the pain and loss*

*I feel for being so naïve continues to be a part of my agony. In retrospect, I guess I didn't really want to know or care to find out the real truth behind his excuses and broken promises. I was determined to have him at any cost and believed his stories without question. In the beginning, we saw each other weekly—first-class hotels, evening strolls, and champagne. He provided it all. I knew he was married, but he explained that his wife was ill, that his marriage was strained, and there was nothing left. But the stories he told turned out to be as phony as he was.*

*When I finally decided to hire a private detective to check on him, I discovered that his wife, far from being sick and confined to a wheelchair, was actually very active and athletic—an avid tennis player. How blind I had been and how connected to his lies, charm, and money. What a fool I was. I ended the affair, but picking up the pieces hasn't been easy. He is still with his wife and undoubtedly fooling around with someone else.*

*For all of the mistresses who have walked in my shoes, my words are simple: find another pair of shoes that fit better, are reliable, and are not on hold. There's nothing worse than buying a nice-looking but cheap pair of shoes, then watching them fall apart after a few weeks.*

Society tends to denigrate the mistress or "other man." Typically, this position is ridiculed, as many consider the occupant of this side of the triangle to be a cold-hearted, calculating, immoral, and manipulative person with no conscience. What is less understood is what motivates this person—how he or she may enter this role as an escape from real commitment, often from some past hurt or grief.

## The Betrayed Partner

As the spurned spouse or partner, you will undoubtedly experience a staggering blow to your ego and self-esteem. People on the perimeter of your life may view you as the casualty of the affair, the innocent bystander. But this is rarely any comfort. This situation was not your choice, and you did not have the ability to actually prevent it once your spouse or partner decided to pursue an affair. Nevertheless, you will inherit the consequences and feel its full impact as the affair unfolds. The fear of change resulting from your partner's betrayal can become paralyzing and all involving. The potential loss of your marriage, as well as the hurt from further rejection by your mate, is usually a constant threat to your well-being and sense of self.

There may be others who will blame you in some way—"if everything was all right at home she/he never would have strayed." The fact is, however, that even if your marriage or partnership is less than perfect, it was your mate's decision to go outside the relationship for solace. Many people have unhappy relationships but never have affairs. Instead, they choose not to begin a new relationship until they are free to pursue one.

## The Children

Infidelity always hurts children, no matter what their age or level of maturity. Even very young children can sense when something is not right. They are very sensitive to the atmosphere in the home and often realize much more than their parents give them credit for—or care to admit. Any changes in the household routine, such as a father who isn't home for dinner much any more, or a mother who seems too preoccupied to read bedtime stories at night, can leave children unsettled.

Once an affair is exposed, children are torn between their loyalties and love for each parent. In some cases, they may blame themselves. Often, they are ashamed of their parents' behavior and may suffer in silence, keeping this knowledge to themselves, rather than sharing it with their best friends or younger siblings. This secrecy is a terrible burden on youngsters, and their fears, concerns, and frustrations can lead to angry and rebellious behavior. Out of nowhere, they may become disciplinary problems or begin to get poor grades in school.

Children truly are the real victims in this situation. I've witnessed the struggles and confusion that confront teenagers, as well as the impact affairs have on their younger brothers and sisters. For all of them, the pain is deep seated, heartfelt, and possibly life long. Take the case of Margaret:

*Margaret's parents divorced when she was ten. She moved into a new home with her mother and was shifted to a new school, which separated her from her friends. She did not adjust well to her surroundings, and a few years later, Margaret had to change schools again because of disciplinary problems. When Margaret was fifteen, her mother remarried. This time to a man who was much younger than she was; in fact, he was closer in age to Margaret. But it was not a marriage made in heaven, and the home soon became a haven of physical and emotional abuse. As a result, Margaret suffered a nervous breakdown and had to be hospitalized.*

*Eventually, Margaret returned home, and began attending college — the same one her mother had gone to years before. The professor of one of her courses seemed very interested in Margaret and quizzed her relentlessly about herself as well as her mother. When she told her mother about the professor's obsessive interest, she learned that her mother had had an affair with this man many years before and had been instrumental in breaking up his marriage. Because of their unusual last name, the professor suspected a relationship between Margaret and the woman in his past.*

*When her mother's second marriage finally ended in divorce, Margaret had to testify to the violence in the home. For years, she continued to suffer from various psychological problems. As an adult, Margaret herself was plagued by one-night stands, two divorces, and a number of illicit affairs.*

Affairs also have a devastating effect on children in terms of trust. When a child learns that one of his or her parents has betrayed the other, it sends the message that nothing in the world is entirely reliable or trustworthy. This also contradicts the lessons they have been taught on the importance of honesty. The impact of infidelity on children is further discussed in Chapter 6, "Through the Eyes of a Child."

## The Extended Family

Branching out from the nuclear family are the parents, siblings, aunts, uncles, cousins, and the in-laws. It doesn't matter whether they're blood relatives or not, any family member close enough to those involved in the affair or the betrayed party will be affected by what is going on. They may offer advice and try to help by bringing the situation under control, but the backlash is inevitable. Holidays and family gatherings, once warm and harmonious, will be strained and uncomfortable, or they won't take place at all.

Family members may take different sides and begin bickering among themselves. Advice may be perceived as meddling. Interference becomes a tactical maneuver on the part of families who ideally should remain neutral. Distance and discretion are particularly important. Take the following story:

> *Jack is a soft-spoken man in his early thirties who has been in a committed relationship for nearly a decade. He knows all about family members having affairs. When he was a teenager, he realized that his brother's wife was becoming much too friendly with his brother's best friend, Danny. Did his brother notice? "I don't think he did," says Jack. "He was busy and involved in the various things he was doing. He almost seemed relieved that my sister-in-law wasn't making demands on him and was leaning more on Danny, asking him to help her out with the things she'd normally be nagging my brother to do. I was aware of all the*

*flirting, when I caught them in a passionate embrace one afternoon, I was sure something was going on."*

When Jack finally told his brother of his suspicions, there was a huge confrontation between the three main players in the affair. His brother and sister-in-law eventually divorced, but only after a long period of upheaval and ill feelings within the family. For years, Jack was guilt ridden and blamed his interference for the all of the unhappiness. Later, as he matured, he realized that he had been put in an untenable position—one in which no person should have to be. The damage to the family unit, however, was never repaired.

Family members may believe they are acting in the best interests of the family unit, but their interference can have harmful ramifications. Of course, withholding such information can have negative repercussions as well. To tell or not to tell? The bottom line is that those who find themselves privy to knowledge about an affair's existence also typically find themselves caught in a no-win situation.

## Friends

Good friends are there when we need them, in good times and bad. Confiding to a friend about an adulterous situation, however, pushes the limits of friendship. Commonly used to validate one's participation in an affair and to share the most tantalizing intimacies that the relationship brings, friends are also a helpful source of alibis and excuses to keep an affair afloat. But even in the best of friendships, people will, at some point, put their own needs ahead of their needy friends. Not only is it difficult to rely on friends for daily support, it's also a heavy burden to place on them. In many cases, people develop close relationships with both parties in a marriage, so when they are asked to take sides or shift allegiances, the friendship is likely to become strained.

*Emily and I have been friends forever. We're both married. A few weeks ago, we met at our usual spot for lunch, but she seemed on edge, secretive, preoccupied. She said she had an important secret to share with me. In the utmost confidentiality, she told me that she was having an affair.*

*I know we've always shared all of our secrets, but why did she have to tell me this? Her husband was my friend, too, and it broke my heart to think of the deception that was going on behind his back.*

*Now I know much more than I want to, and this whole ordeal has upset me greatly. The worst part is that I have nobody to discuss my feelings with except Emily, and she believes her affair is justified in some way. I disagree and we argue. I don't know what to do. This has put a real strain on our friendship. Most upsetting, I find myself in a moral dilemma: is it fair for me to let her husband continue to be betrayed? What should I do?*

The role of confidante, advisor, ally, or alibi can become draining and tiring, and eventually this strain is likely to damage what was once a healthy friendship. This pressure often results in the friendship's demise—yet another painful consequence of infidelity.

## Employers and Colleagues

As the complexities of an affair begin to overtake one's daily life, job performance nearly always suffers. Continuous daydreaming brought on by the "romance" commonly causes lack of concentration at work. Job focus takes a back seat to thoughts that are more apt to center on how and when the next tryst will occur, or what excuses or alibis might work for future liaisons. Such obsessing can put a serious strain on anyone's ability to be an effective worker. And it won't take long for colleagues to realize that one of their coworkers isn't pulling his or her weight. Sure, they may not mind covering once in a while, but eventually their tolerance will turn to resentment. And let's not forget about bosses, who tend to have zero tolerance for ineffective job performance.

Affairs are also common between coworkers. When love makes its way into the workplace, a new set of problems can crop up, as seen in the following story:

> *Barry and Susan worked together. Both were bored with their marriages. After several months of flirting, they began to have regular lunchtime trysts. Shortly after their affair had begun, they resolved to tell their respective spouses that they each wanted a divorce. They decided to break the news to their partners on the weekend. Susan told her husband that she wanted out of the marriage, but when she got to work on Monday, she learned that Barry had changed his mind. Susan was furious. She also felt panic at the thought of how she had put her own marriage at risk. Trying to save face and salvage her marriage (and get back at her lover), she claimed that she had been sexually harassed by Barry. Susan's husband was enraged, and he encouraged Susan to file suit against Barry. After months of conflict and distress, the dust eventually settled. Susan was reassigned to a dead-end job. Barry was fired.*

Whether or not your affair involves someone at work, eventually people in the workplace will become irritated at having to deal with your personal life. Even if they don't know the real reasons for your faltering performance and are merely guessing, employers and colleagues eventually face the difficult question of what to do about a situation that is affecting them. You may find yourself ostracized, demoted, or even fired.

## Lawyers

Affairs cost money. Divorce costs more money. Legal fees are a considerable expense to add to the already rising cost of having an affair. It's wise to consider the legal and financial consequences before passion, hormones, and romance take over. Visit a divorce court (if you dare) or check out some of the movies that show the ramifications of breakups. *Kramer vs. Kramer, The War of the Roses,* and *The First Wives Club* are just a few of the numerous realistic accounts, fictional or not, of failed marriages. Take a lesson from people you know who have gone through divorce. Pay attention to the consequences of others.

Remember, lawyers get paid first, usually at the expense of both spouses. The more acrimonious and drawn out the divorce proceedings are, the larger the chunk of money the lawyers take.

## Accountants

When significant assets are fought over as a result of an affair, after the lawyers, accountants are usually next in line for payment. One thing is certain—taxes must still be paid whether you're married or not. The Internal Revenue Service has no interest in the details of relationships. It cares only about getting its money.

## Caregivers

Counselors. Therapists. Doctors. Clergy. Teachers. These are only some of the people who may get involved as a marriage breaks up. Often they can and are willing to give support, but in many cases, their help involves payment.

## Others

Private detectives. Police. Neighbors. Florists. Secretaries. Hotel desk clerks. Maitre D's. There are a number of people you would never suspect who can be drawn into the life of an affair, often to provide lies, alibis, or excuses. You may consider some of these people trusted aides or allies who help keep the secret of your affair, but they can also do more harm than you may realize. Sure, they may pass on messages for you or turn a blind eye to your trysts, but if they are called upon to testify in divorce proceedings, in all likelihood, they will not perjure themselves.

## RARELY A PRIVATE MATTER

Although extramarital affairs usually can be kept secret, especially in the beginning, eventually they will be discovered, and often sooner than later. Getting caught may even be a hidden agenda of one or both of the participants. The person who discovers the relationship and when will differ from affair to affair, but don't fool yourself into believing it won't happen. The odds are very high that the wall of secrecy surrounding any affair eventually will come tumbling down.

Lies and affairs go hand in hand—they are usually the best way to camouflage the situation and keep people off track, at least for a while. Some experts suggest that keeping the affair hidden from the betrayed spouse is a wise course. "Letting it all hang out" in an effort to be absolved is really a callous means of hurting the spouse or partner. Others feel total honesty is the only route. Again, this varies between couples and across situations. But many who have been in affairs have, at some point, felt compelled to tell the world, including the betrayed partner. Just remember that nobody likes knowing they have been lied to and duped.

Regardless of your role in the triangle, there will probably be a point at which you are going to want to tell someone about it. You'll want to share or to confide what you're going through. Often this begins with close friends and individuals you trust. Additionally, sharing your secret is also a way to enlist their help and cooperation—for cover-up alibis, as well as validation for the affair itself. The betrayed partner will also feel a need to vent his or her feelings, and before you know it, the word is out. This leads to gossip and rumors, and eventually the number of people who learn of and are affected by the affair can be staggering.

## A BOUQUET OF CONSEQUENCES

Affairs are never as simple as they appear at the onset. Although they may begin innocuously enough, with time, their effects can become overwhelming. In the end, they often become more complicated than you ever could have imagined possible at the start. Unfortunately, if you are just flirting with the idea of betrayal, you are probably not interested in the reasons why you shouldn't. I know that I wasn't. But I should have been. Personal integrity is often the first to go as hypocrisy, lies, and deception—all common to extramarital affairs—begin to unfold.

Affairs have a profound effect on all of those involved, both emotionally and physically. A "broken heart" may seem like only a figure of speech, but in reality there is a real sensation of physical pain that accompanies the end of a marriage or partnership or love affair. I know whereof I speak. It happens. It hurts. And it can happen to you. Hearts break when someone you love leaves, when someone you love betrays you, or when you've been unfaithful to the one you love. A broken heart can feel irreparable, but it helps to know that it does mend with time. Nevertheless, for a long time, anyone touched by an affair can feel as though a dark, melancholy cloud has descended. For some, these feelings of grief and loss can result in clinical depression, requiring medical assistance and possibly medication. This black cloud can extend to children and extended family members, as well as close friends.

Those affected by the lies suffer the emotional and spiritual violations of being willfully used. Even the lover can end up feeling like a commodity, serving a purpose, but usually of secondary importance to the married partner. I've seen children become disillusioned as the people they love and admire the most are revealed to be selfish and uncaring, all consumed by the details of their affairs. Worse, they may feel responsible for a parent's infidelity and somehow think it is their fault. Or, as adults, they may tend to repeat the cycle of unfaithfulness.

I've seen extended family members forced to take sides in disputes between the people they love—creating situations in which family ties are lost. Financial devastation is another realistic consequence of an affair. In the workplace, employers often find themselves standing by helplessly as otherwise good employees stop producing, leaving resentful colleagues to pick up the slack. In the case of affairs within the workplace, the most dedicated of individuals may find their livelihood jeopardized. And if, by chance, sexual harassment enters the picture, the professional consequences can be devastating for everyone.

## "I SHOULD HAVE SEEN IT COMING."

People who live together should know each other well. Before having proof of an affair, the betrayed partner is likely to go through a period of suspicion, one in which he or she may catch the partner in a lie, or begin to notice altered behavior patterns.

If you suspect your partner may be involved in an affair, heed the warning signs. The usual reason that the betrayed one is often "the last to know" is due to a steadfast denial or refusal to believe there may be problems in the relationship. If your partner expresses dissatisfaction with your relationship, listen. Don't brush it off. This is a clue that things are not all right. Pay attention to what is going on around you. If you suspect that your partner or spouse is cheating, *trust your suspicions.* How's your spouse's track record when it comes to trust? Do you know? Unless you are the type of person who *usually* is unjustly suspicious of your partner's fidelity, chances are you may have good reason to think he or she is betraying you now. You owe it to yourself and to your family to find out for certain *before* a possible confrontation.

If your partner is having an affair, there's a good chance that there will be a number of red flags flying—the most obvious of which is *changed behavior.* Any discernible change on the part of your partner can be a sign of guilt. For example, is

# Geographical Factors and Affairs

*Although people all over the country and throughout the world engage in adulterous behavior, geographical factors do play a part in how an affair plays out, and, potentially, in how the judge and/or jury view the case. Different parts of the United States, for instance, tend to have varying "standards" for determining the extent to which infidelity is "officially" tolerated. For instance, what may be thought of as a common and ordinary occurrence in certain locations on the East or West Coast may be considered scandalous and immoral in certain parts of the South and the Midwest. And while affairs may be perceived as part of the everyday hustle and bustle in a busy urban setting, they may be viewed as a major scandal in a small rural community. This isn't to say that affairs don't happen in places where there is ostensibly zero-tolerance, but it does mean that they are undertaken much more secretively and covertly, and may have more devastating ramifications.*

*Furthermore, some cultures view infidelity differently from the way it is perceived in our society. For instance, in places such as Japan and a number of Middle Eastern countries, a man's infidelity is both tolerated and expected.*

your spouse or partner, who normally doesn't even remember your birthday, suddenly lavishing you with gifts or paying an excessive amount of attention to you? On the other hand, is he or she suddenly displaying signs of indifference toward you and your relationship? Is your partner becoming withdrawn and silent, less communicative and open than normal? The following signs also may be indications that your partner is having an affair:

• *Mood swings.* Is your partner suddenly quick to get angry or have wild and significant mood extremes? Does he or she seem more impatient and irritated by things that never seemed bothersome before?

- *Criticism.* Is your partner suddenly critical of you and/or the children?

- *A change in sexual patterns.* Have you noticed a difference in your intimate time together? Is your mate suddenly withdrawn sexually or, on the contrary, more attentive? For years, people believed that if the physical side of marriage was working well, people wouldn't stray, or if people had an affair, they would lose interest in their spouse. The truth is, for some people, an affair is so stimulating sexually that sex within the marriage also increases.

- *Increased work hours.* Is your partner working longer hours than usual, or taking an increased number of business trips all of a sudden? Is he or she on the phone at odd hours discussing "meetings" or "unfinished projects"?

- *Impromptu absences.* Is your partner suddenly running an increased number of errands that take him or her away from home?

- *Mysterious phone calls.* When talking on the phone, does your partner sometimes lower his or her voice or display unusual body language?

In addition to these red flags, there are other signs to watch for:

- *Scent.* It's the oldest sign in the book. If you think you smell someone else's body scent on your partner or on his or her clothes, your suspicions of infidelity may be right. Lipstick is another smoking gun. Where there is lipstick, there was once a pair of lips. The smell of someone else's perfume or cologne is another giveaway.

- *A new communication system.* Has your partner installed

password-protected voicemail or e-mail on your home computer? Has he or she suddenly decided that you need "call waiting" on your phone line? Such technological systems are a real boon for adulterous relationships. It is not uncommon for an unfaithful spouse to set up a special e-mail account with a different provider from the one the family uses. This allows freedom to communicate privately with a lover. Does your spouse stop reading e-mail as soon as you walk into the room? These are all signs that something might be going on. (Caller ID, by the way, is one very common means for lovers to get caught these days.)

- *Changes in appearance.* Does your partner seem to be taking an interest in exercise all of a sudden? Are clothing and grooming taking on new importance? Does he or she seem to be taking a lot more time getting dressed for work than usual?

- *Personal accounts.* Have you discovered a new bank account or credit card in your spouse's name? Are bills sent to the office that used to come to the home? Do you accidentally find mail or credit card receipts that have been hidden?

- *Lack of funds.* Does money seem tighter than usual? Are funds dwindling for no apparent reason? Do you know where all the financial accounts are kept and their balances?

- *Lies and deception.* Is your mate deceitful about seemingly innocuous matters? Lying is habit-forming, and those who lie to hide a part of their lives in a careful, well-calculated way, often begin to lie impulsively about insignificant, unrelated matters as well. People also contradict themselves when they lie. As Mark Twain said, "You need a good memory to be a liar." Have you discovered inconsistencies in your partner's stories?

- *Family history.* People tend to repeat patterns they have experienced. Did someone in your partner's family have an affair? What was your partner's reaction to it? Did he or she treat it as unimportant? If so, consider this an important warning sign. Those who do not take affairs seriously may well be prone to having one themselves.

Remember, nobody wants to believe that his or her partner is unfaithful, but denying that which is obvious has its own set of damaging ramifications. It is only after the reality of infidelity has been faced that healing can begin to occur.

## SUMMING IT UP

What may have seemed to be a simple, uncomplicated fling at the start, is likely to transform into one of the most complex situations in a person's life. If you are currently involved in an affair, you probably believe your behavior is well hidden and that you are immune to the usual damaging ramifications of infidelity. Undoubtedly, you think your situation is different (most do), and somehow feel that your secret will remain just that. It is important for you to understand that your beliefs are typical, however, they are not realistic. In the next chapter, you will discover the reality.

# 4

# So You Think You're Different?

*"Like the bee sting, the promiscuous leave behind them in each encounter something of themselves by which they are made to suffer."*

—Cyril Connolly
*The Unquiet Grave,* 1945

It's human nature for people to view themselves as unique. Individual. Unlike everyone else. To some extent, of course, this is true. We are all shaped by experiences in life that make us different from one another. No two people feel or see things *exactly* the same way. This truth, however, should not blind us to the many similarities we share.

If your life has been touched by an affair, you probably believe that your situation is like no other. No one could possibly feel the same way you are feeling. Regardless of the cause or catalyst for your involvement, or the side of the triangle you occupy, you are likely to feel that no one else has ever loved like this before, or been hurt like this before, or been so justified in this kind of involvement before. Guess what. They have. Matter of fact, you'll probably be surprised at just how much commonality actually exists between the roles and the behaviors typically displayed during the life cycles of affairs.

As you will see in this chapter, it doesn't matter what role you claim in the love triangle—the betrayed spouse, the cheating wife or husband, or the "other" man or woman. It makes no difference if you are male or female, young or old, gay or straight. These roles, by their very nature, are fraught with similarities. In other words, you're not one *in* a million; rather you're one *of* millions.

## WOMEN AND MEN AND RELATIONSHIPS

When it comes to love and relationships, there are a number of basic behavioral commonalities and differences among the sexes. Through well-documented research, as well as countless hours spent interacting with men and women in workshops and support groups, I have become well-aware of some of these common gender characteristics.

In many ways, men and women are actually far more alike than they are different; other than a single chromosome, basically we differ very little. But society views and treats us quite differently from the time we are born. And when it comes to affairs, men tend to behave in a certain way, while women tend to behave in another. Of course, I am speaking in generalities when discussing gender likenesses and differences. The reality is, as you will see, that for as different as men and women can be, that's how similarly they can react when they occupy the same side of a love triangle.

Men, at least according to the data compiled from a number of studies and questionnaires, admit to having more affairs than women. Two-thirds of married men and close to half of married women in the United States have admitted to involvement in extramarital affairs. Based on the 1980s research of Shere Hite in *Women and Love* (New York: St. Martin's Press, 1989), "The likelihood of a woman having an affair increases precipitously after five years of marriage." According to Hite, 13 percent of women are unfaithful during their first two years of marriage. After five years, this percentage jumps as high as 75 percent. In comparison, twenty-some years earlier in 1963, the famous Kinsey Report reported that 26 percent of married women

admitted to having affairs after five years. Hite found nearly three times that number. Men's rate of extramarital sex
also doubled during that same period, to 75 percent according to Hite. What these numbers indicate is that infidelity is
a serious problem for men and women alike, and appears to
be on the rise.

Although it's impossible to predict exactly how anyone
will behave in a relationship, there are a few generalizations
about women and men that seem to hold true. For instance,
when it comes to falling in love, women typically lead with
their hearts, although they tend not to make impulsive decisions. A woman's desire to feel loved and appreciated is usually an important prerequisite before she engages in sex, and
she flirts with the idea of having an affair long before she
actually has one. Generally speaking, women are driven by
the need to find that perfect fit, the ideal companion ("Mr.
Right"), and to find the happy ending to the fairy-tale life
they were promised in books and movies.

Women who are involved in amorous relationships of any
kind tend to be consumed by them totally. Suddenly, they
find it difficult to maintain focus in their daily lives, especially at the onset of the relationship. They become unorganized
and seem to float through their days, daydreaming of their
lovers and exhibiting other "classic" signs of being in love.
They also tend to analyze and dissect their love lives, viewing
them from every possible angle. Stereotypically, women feel
the need to share their sexual involvements (both in and out
of affairs) at length with trusted friends, seeking validation
for their behavior.

The actions of men, on the other hand, are often led by
their desire for sex. It's usually sex first, then, perhaps, love
may enter the picture. For the most part, men are not as ana-
lytical as women about their relationships. They tend to
accept their involvements at face value and refrain from sharing or overanalyzing their emotions and behaviors. They also
find it easier than women to replace one sexual partner with
another.

## AFFAIRS AND ROLE SIMILARITIES

Now that you are aware of certain basic likenesses and differences between men and women, let's take a closer look at the various roles of an affair—the cheating spouse, the "other" man or woman, and the betrayed partner—and see just how much commonality exists within each one.

### The Cheating Partner

Although I discuss "married" couples in this section, I am actually referring to anyone who is involved in a committed monogamous relationship of any kind.

One of the most striking differences between married men and women having affairs is in the degree of satisfaction each reports in their relationships. In rather sexist fashion, people in our society tend to think that men stray when they are not happy at home, when they're not getting the love and support (and sex) they want and expect from their wives. However, according to one study, over half of the men who admitted to infidelity claimed they had happy, stable marriages. Only 34 percent of the women in the same study made the same claim. "Most women believe that if you love your partner you wouldn't even be interested in an affair," says Baltimore psychologist Shirley Glass, in an article that appeared in *Psychology Today*. Dr. Glass' research confirmed that even men who are perfectly happy at home have affairs.

Emotional intimacy and sex do not necessarily go hand-in-hand for most married men. They seem able to separate their home lives and their infidelities without much trouble. In fact, Glass found that men in long-term marriages who were having affairs often reported that they were very satisfied with their partners. Married women having affairs, on the other hand, said the opposite. They were not happy in their married lives and were looking for something that was missing.

I believe this reflects fairly accurately the types of roles that men and women take on in relationships. Women have "emotional" affairs and men have "sexual" relationships outside marriage. As discussed earlier, women, by their very nature, tend to fall in love first, then decide to have sex, while men go for sex and then possibly fall in love. Many married men have reportedly entered affairs out of passion and a desire for conquest, enjoying the thrill of the chase, like a game. Many conduct themselves in a detached, cavalier way, especially at the onset. They believe they won't get caught and their emotions won't be engaged. For the most part, cheating husbands are not interested in why an affair started, why it continues, why it is hurtful, and why it must end.

One interesting similarity among both husbands and wives is that neither considers physical intimacy with a person of the same sex infidelity.

*Carol and Phil, the parents of three young children, seemed to have a great marriage. Carol was an obstetrician/gynecologist, and Phil was an information-services consultant—a job that kept him hopping throughout the country on business trips. Carol's friend Marsha was an abused wife. One night when Phil was away on a trip, Marsha showed up at the front door with a black eye and bloodied lip. Carol ushered her inside, and insisted that Marsha stay in the guest room until she was able to make other arrangements.*

*A few nights later, when one of the children scampered into Carol's bed to escape the fright of a nightmare, she found Marsha in the bed also. When questioned, Carol explained that she was having a "sleep-over" with her friend. Her daughter accepted the explanation, but couldn't wait to tell Daddy when he got back from his trip. Actually, Carol and Marsha were having an affair.*

*Phil had always noticed the closeness of the two women, and may even have suspected them of being more than "just friends" in the past, but he always talked himself out of his suspicions. When he confronted Carol, she admitted being intimate with Marsha, but insisted it shouldn't affect their marriage. After all, it wasn't like she was having an affair with another man! She refused to discuss it further. Phil filed for divorce, which threw the family into a state of turmoil that lasted for many years.*

Unfaithful wives display further unique behaviors that differ from men in the same situation. For instance, married women tend to tolerate their unhappiness and the dysfunction in a marriage long before considering an extramarital affair, while men are quicker to enter an affair as a way of handling the same stressors. And unlike married men, who are reluctant to seek therapy or counseling to strengthen the weaknesses in a failing marriage, women are more inclined to seek such outside help. (Husbands often agree to counseling only as a last resort to keep peace within the household.) Finally, wives appear more guilt-ridden about their infidelity than their straying husbands.

Husbands often look for different qualities in their lovers than they desire in their wives. For example, a man whose spouse is a strong career woman, may look for a more domestic, dependent person with whom to have an affair. The following story exemplifies this.

*Robert is a tall, sandy-haired man in his early forties. An associate professor of microbiology at a prominent university, Robert met and married Mandy when they were both in their twenties. For many years, they seemed to have a wonderful life: they were both educated and attractive with fulfilling careers. They also had two beautiful children and a nanny. Robert, however, eventually began to feel as if something was missing in his marriage. He and Mandy didn't seem to talk any more, and their intimate times together were becoming less frequent. Both were preoccupied, too tired, too busy.*

*On the other hand, Valerie, the children's nanny, was always there. When Robert came home from work, she had dinner on the table; the kids were always bathed and ready for bed. She'd talk to him about his day and seemed genuinely interested in his work. She sympathized with him and the difficulties he was having with a few of his colleagues—difficulties that were standing in the way of his promotion to Department Chairman. In spite of their twenty-year age difference, Robert felt that he and Valerie had a lot in common. One day, while Mandy was off on a business trip, it seemed perfectly natural for Robert to kiss Valerie. Then things continued in the bedroom.*

*For several months, the affair lent spice to Robert's life, making him feel complete. He bought little gifts for Valerie—and for Mandy too. He felt expansive and warm towards the world. Even his sex life with Mandy improved; the more sensual and passionate he felt with Valerie, the more desire he seemed to have for his wife.*

*One day, Robert's daughter walked in on them in the bedroom. Quite innocently, she told her mother that she saw Daddy and Nanny cuddling in bed. When Mandy confronted Robert, he confessed all. Valerie was fired immediately and returned to her home in another state. Robert lost his wife, children, and much of his income in an ugly divorce. The colleagues Robert had been having trouble with used his infidelity as proof of his unreliability, and he never got that promotion.*

Married men are also inclined to deny their infidelity, even if they get caught in the act. As comedian Lenny Bruce once advised cheating husbands, "Never tell! Not if you love your wife (and most men do). In fact, if [she] walks in on you when you're in the act, deny it. Yeah, just flat out deny it and she'll believe it. . . . Just say, 'Honey, this chick came downstairs with a sign around her neck: *Lay on top of me or I'll die. What else could I do?'*" It is also common for cheating spouses to blame their partners for their unfaithfulness.

As mentioned previously, women, by their very nature, often feel the need to discuss the intimacies of their lives (including affairs) with trusted friends. Married men, on the other hand, try to keep their indiscretions secret, telling as few people as possible. They tend to divulge their affairs only to a select group of people, such as those who are needed to provide alibis.

Men also underestimate their wives' reactions to their infidelities, and don't expect their marriages to end over an affair. They are shocked if they are asked to leave the home immediately. Often they will claim an affair is over, even when it isn't and they have no intention of ending it. They consider an apology to their wives and perhaps an expensive gift or two to be sufficient atonement. Husbands are the ones who usually bear the financial brunt of an affair and its possible consequences, such as alimony, legal fees, and child support.

It doesn't matter if you are the cheating husband or the unfaithful wife, as the married player in an affair, it is you who will be expected to handle the infidelity and its consequences. The burden will be on you to cope with two separate relationships and ensure that they are kept separate. And it is you who will be faced with the pressure of fulfilling two sets of expectations—your spouse's and your lover's. Keeping the affair under wraps lands squarely on your shoulders, and they best be broad!

Once an affair is discovered, what generally follows is an endless round of recriminations, anger, resentment, and rancor, shattered vows and broken marriages. Cheating spouses generally find themselves powerless to protect their most treasured assets, both tangible and intangible. Marriages, families, careers, bank accounts, investments, houses, furniture, reputations, good will, and friendships are all on the line as a direct result of infidelity. Often, unfaithful partners are powerless and can only sit by and watch as the world around them crumbles.

## The "Other" Man or Woman

Those who play the role of the "other" man or woman are

simply one of many who have found themselves in love with the right person (or so they believe) at the wrong time. The most controversial side of the triangle, unmarried lovers are associated with the greatest number of stereotypes—home wrecker, troublemaker, thief, snake in the grass—and they are the objects of intense gossip and speculation. They are considered selfish, manipulative, and, of course, immoral, and the world tends to blame them for an affair's existence.

This role is also viewed as the most thrilling, passionate, frustrating, and isolated side of the triangle. Its participants are typically at the mercy of their married lovers. Although they are "on call" most of the time, and are on the receiving end of broken dates and promises, their lovers will continue to insist they come first. They feel privy to confidential information that could ultimately destroy their lovers as well as their families, and they consider themselves important because of this knowledge.

Most participants in this role idealize their lovers, viewing them through rose-colored glasses. They don't care to see them as deceivers—people who lie to their partners as they lead double lives with divided hearts. Rather, they blot out these uncomfortable truths, and convince themselves that their lovers are sincere people who are, perhaps, caught up in a poor marriage or miserable home situation. They rarely, if ever, consider the possibility that if their lovers cheat on their spouses, they may cheat on them as well. (They feel that they are all their lovers need.) They also believe their lovers are always honest with them, and often assume that the marriage was in trouble before the affair began. In addition, those who find themselves in the role of either the other man or woman characteristically feel justified in their affairs, accepting little or no responsibility for any problems that the relationship may cause in their lover's marriage. And they believe if the affair ends, their lover would be with someone else. So they continue to excuse their behavior, feeling very connected to their lovers.

Unmarried lovers tend to view their affairs as sophisticated relationships, and they seem to bond emotionally to their married lovers through the stories and details they share. They don't realize how little they actually know. A mistress rarely considers that her "in-the-bedroom" view of her lover is really nothing more than a romanticized "snapshot" of what he (or she) is really like. She has no idea what it is like to live with this person on a daily basis, and spends a lot of time obsessing about him and his life—much of which is based on fantasy, not reality.

The simple fact that their lovers are married puts mistresses and other unmarried lovers in very vulnerable and uncertain positions. They tend to trust (at least in the beginning of the affair) everything their married partners tell them—including the fact that they are number one. They also sincerely believe that their married lovers are committed to them, that their relationship is special. As an affair escalates, there comes a point at which the unmarried lovers become very possessive of their married paramours, believing that they belong more to them than they do to their spouses. They are certain that their lovers would choose to be with them if there wasn't a husband or wife blocking the way. Commonly, they envision themselves as the new spouse. The reality, however, is that most married players are more likely to end their affairs rather than lose the years of equity that have built up in their marriages.

*I still can't believe that I was able to create such a nightmare. I worked for my sister's husband as his secretary. I have always been close to my sister and her family, and through work, I also became extremely close to my brother-in-law. Working together every day, our relationship developed into more than that of a boss and worker. We couldn't deny the sexual attraction we felt for each other, and eventually we became intimate. During our affair, he constantly told me how unhappy he was in his marriage and that he was going to leave my sister so we could be together. Even though I felt guilty and ashamed of what I was doing,*

*I was in love with him and thought he was worth it. And after all, why should he stay in a marriage if he wasn't happy? This rationalization prompted me to maintain the affair for many years.*

*But as time progressed, I wanted him all to myself. I finally threatened him—he had to leave my sister or I would tell her about the affair myself. He refused, saying it was a bad time. He claimed it was too close to the holidays, and with the children . . . blah blah blah. It was just another excuse in a long line of excuses. Deep in my heart, I knew he had no intention of ever breaking up with my sister, so I decided to go through with my threat and tell her myself.*

*Well, my actions blew up in my face. Sure, my sister was pretty angry with her husband, but she was absolutely furious with me and blamed me for everything. She accused me of being the one who lured him into the affair. My brother-in-law stopped seeing me immediately, and, of course, I lost my job. The two of them stayed together and shut me out of their lives completely. No longer was I a part of holidays and other family functions. I wasn't even allowed to see my nieces any more.*

*I lost my job, my sister, my nieces, and my lover. The entire family blamed me while my brother-in-law got off scot-free. How I wish I had never said anything, but at the time, I thought it was the right thing to do.*

Despite the risks and consequences, the other man or woman will usually choose to stay in the affair. As seen in the case above, an unmarried lover will eventually tire of his or her position in the background and issue an ultimatum, threatening to end the affair unless the married lover has left his or her spouse. The outcome is usually predictable—the married lover maintains relationships with *both* spouse and lover. And even when a lover's threat is realized and the affair ends, it's often only temporary. When lovers open their eyes to the reality of their "second best" status in the affair, the common tendency is to hang onto their married lovers even tighter, believing that the pain of letting go will hurt even more. They seem to reject the idea of counseling or therapy to help them cope with an affair, and in some cases want to have the affair exposed when their patience wears out.

In most instances, the other man or woman is not threatened by a married lover's spouse, even if intimacy still exists within the marriage. (After all, aren't lovers more important than spouses?) Instead, they are more likely to feel threatened by a lover's children, whom they believe are stronger incentives for keeping the marriage intact. And although they may toy with the idea of confronting a lover's spouse, they usually don't.

Both single men and women who are involved with married individuals seem to have similar motivations. For instance, some people who fear commitment are sometimes drawn to those who are already married. Persons already in committed relationships are less likely to press their lovers for more.

> *Never married, thirty-two-year-old Ken thrives on having affairs with married women. He makes no bones about this, telling his buddies that he needs to be free of commitment. Relationships with married women allow him to enjoy the best of both worlds. Ken feels that married women are better sexual partners — more experienced, less inhibited, and well seasoned. He is quite open about the excitement and diversion married women have brought to his life. They present fewer obstacles all around. Ken is often relieved when his lover has to go home to her husband. This gives him time to spend on his hobbies, to enjoy his friends, and, sometimes, to date other women (which, of course, his lovers never know about). No responsibility. No pressure. For Ken, this is having it all.*

Some people who fall in love with those who are married are seduced by tales of woe or abuse. They see themselves as knights in shining armor or fairy godmothers—determined to "save" the mistreated ones. And then there are those gigolos or playgirls, who allow themselves to be "kept" by married lovers. They provide sex and companionship in exchange for gifts and money.

Regardless of the exploitation and controversy surrounding this role, getting involved with a married person comes with a high cost in emotions and precious time. Eventually, those who find themselves in this situation will be faced with the decision either to accept the terms and consequences of the relationship or to become involved with someone else who is unattached and available.

## The Betrayed Partner

Of the three major players in a love triangle, the betrayed spouse is the one most likely to be viewed as the innocent one—a sad casualty of the affair. After all, the betrayed wife had no say in her husband's tryst with his secretary, and the betrayed husband wasn't consulted by his wife before she became involved with her tennis instructor. Of course, there will be those who consider betrayed spouses as "causes" of their partners' infidelity—"If he had paid more attention to her . . ." "If she hadn't nagged him so much . . ." Generally speaking, however, these people receive the most sympathy and compassion from the people around them.

Many women who discover their husbands are having an affair initially react with shock and disbelief, but after the initial heartbreaking reality has set in, anger typically takes over. The wife who is cheated on is likely to feel bitter resentment over the fact that her husband has been emotionally intimate with someone else—that he has shared his thoughts, secrets, and emotions with another person. There is the possibility that he has divulged personal information about their marriage and family. To her, the affair is more than physical intimacy; it is a violation of their relationship, of their love, of that exclusive bond.

Generally speaking, men tend to have less suspicious

natures than their counterparts, and they aren't as likely to suspect their partners of cheating. A man who discovers his wife's affair initially reacts with shock and anger. He feels betrayed at the mere thought of her having sex with another man (even if he himself has been unfaithful at some point in the relationship). As writer and humorist Quentin Crisp once said, "As we all know from witnessing the consuming jealousy of husbands who are never faithful, people do not confine themselves to the emotions to which they are entitled."

Many betrayed spouses may find that they are still in love with their unfaithful partners, but are unwilling to forgive and forget their indiscretions. The bonds of trust have been broken. And even if the marriage remains intact, the affair will undoubtedly be brought up time and again after it has ended. Women frequently tend to dwell in the role of the victims, keeping themselves and their families trapped in the affair by reliving it over and over. As the betrayed ones, they typically refuse to take any responsibility for the behavior of their partners, and most find it difficult to cope with their hurtful emotions. Men in particular rarely give themselves the adequate time they need to sort out their feelings. This commonly results in hasty decisions that are later regretted.

A betrayed woman usually feels the need to discuss her husband's infidelity with trusted friends and family members; she may even seek counseling to get through the pain and possibly salvage the marriage. Most feel the need to have their decisions validated and are likely to spend a great deal of time rallying support from family and friends to back up their positions as the injured parties. A man, on the other hand, usually doesn't feel the same need to discuss his wife's affair with others—it is too humiliating, a crushing blow to his ego and self-esteem.

Both husbands and wives tend to blame the "other" man or woman rather than their own spouses for the extramarital affair. Most women insist on knowing specific details about the affair including information about the "lovers," although they usually find it traumatic dealing with this information.

Historically, a wife is threatened by her spouse's lover and feels the need to put her down to anyone who will listen. She wants to compete with this lover and may become obsessed with her. The betrayed wife usually wants to know what her husband's lover looks like, where she lives and works, and how she spends her free time. She'll want to know how they met and will expect details of their sexual escapades. A wife may call her husband's lover just to hear her voice and then quickly hang up. And although she may want to confront the lover, usually she won't. She may, however, fantasize about doing something terrible (even violent) to her.

A betrayed man, on the other hand, is more likely to actually confront his wife's lover and possibly resort to violence to even the score. He may also become physically abusive to his wife. I have seen a number of otherwise gentle men seethe with rage over their wives' infidelity. A man in one of my support groups who discovered his wife had been having an affair with his best friend and business partner shared, "The pain is unbearable. I want to kill this son of a bitch for trying to ruin my life." A confrontation between the two men resulted in a physical brawl.

Depression, insomnia, and weight loss or gain are some of the common manifestations of the stress felt by betrayed partners. Possibly most difficult, they have to deal with the breach of trust and intimacy brought on by the affair. And although they may want to retain their marriages in spite of the infidelity, they often do not allow themselves to. Affairs are the death knell of many marriages. Those involved in divorce have to find ways to contend with the fallout, including changes in social and financial status, as well as a shift in the dynamics of the family unit. There is a change in the general quality of life. Children often become pawns and are fought over in custody battles.

Wives are usually quicker than their husbands to involve attorneys for counsel ("I'll make him pay!"). Many demote their cheating husbands to the status of a child, and may even take advantage of the situation by placing unreasonable demands on them. Some women use their husbands' affairs as excuses for their own emotional outbursts or any other type of behavior that could be criticized. Betrayed husbands are more likely to inflict psychological warfare on their wives, as well as material penalties. Initially, betrayed wives as well as husbands may demand that their cheating partners leave the house immediately, although the man is more inclined to walk out.

For most married couples, change is difficult, especially when it involves breaking up a family. And as mentioned earlier, cheating husbands and wives are often more inclined to break off their affairs rather than watch their marriages crumble. Affairs usually die before a marriage does.

## MY STORY WASN'T SO DIFFERENT AFTER ALL

As the events of my life unfolded, I believed, as most people do, that my experiences were different from anyone else's. I thought the relationships I developed were special and unique, and to some degree they were; but, as you will see, my behavior and the experiences I encountered both in my marriages as well as in my affairs were typical.

### Starting Over Again

After our daughter's death, I divorced my husband, left California, and moved back to Ohio, where I enrolled in graduate school. Shortly after, I married a man who was nine years my senior. One of the more "eligible" bachelors in Cincinnati, he was a workaholic who was married to his job. During this relatively short relationship, I had a miscarriage, yet another tragic loss for me. I decided to have a tubal ligation to prevent another pregnancy. At the time, I had a rewarding position as the director for a pilot mental health program for school-age children and their families. I loved my work, but not at the expense of my marriage. On the other hand, my husband's devotion to his work was extreme, all-consuming; eventually it drove a wedge between us.

Even though I was living in Ohio, my love for the West Coast frequented my thoughts and I visited California as often as I could. During one visit, I met a man who gave me a reason to leave my husband, leave Ohio, and move back to California. Like my very first marriage, I used this man to escape from the life I had been living. It was a poor choice, and I soon realized we had nothing in common. So, once again, I ended a relationship.

After the breakup, I decided to explore the world of cosmetic surgery. My plastic surgeon—a married man—soon became my lover. To my shock, while in the throes of this affair, I became pregnant again (so much for the tubal ligation!) and suffered another miscarriage. As I went through the trauma of yet another loss, I also experienced one of life's little ironies. I discovered my lover was no more faithful to me than he had been to his wife. I walked in on him unexpectedly one evening and found him in the arms of one of the nurses from the hospital. Later he tried to rationalize his infidelity by blaming me, claiming that I had been distant and indifferent to him since my miscarriage. As discussed earlier in this chapter, my lover's response to getting caught was typical—he blamed *me* for his behavior.

At this point, the affair had simply become too much for me. I ended the relationship, but my stress level mounted and my general good health began to falter. Following the advice of my doctors, I decided to take a long rest to regroup. I had to rethink my life while putting the scattered pieces back together again. It soon became clear that I had to stop running. Throughout my life, most of my energies had been targeted to outside sources, such as my daughter, husbands, lovers, jobs, and schoolwork. Nothing had been left for me. The drama of my life had sustained me and kept me going since my father's death many years before, but this in itself had kept me emotionally disabled. I was not able to focus on who I was or what I wanted; instead, I spent years chasing some elusive dream of love that had kept me immobilized in terms of actual personal growth. I had looked only outward and forward for solutions—more schooling, another husband, a new lover—something or someone with whom I could feel safe and pretend I was okay.

By having affairs and risking what I had, I was also, in some way, "testing" the reality of my life. But it was for the wrong reasons and through the wrong means. Not only did I lose material possessions like cars and houses and jewelry, I also sacrificed other assets like respect, good will, love, and acceptance, as we all do when we allow our lives to spin out of control.

## My Story Continues

I met my fifth husband in quite an unusual way. He noticed me one day while driving on the San Diego Freeway, one of the busiest roads in southern California. He was seven years younger and very soft-spoken. I liked him immediately. A highly successful businessman, he was looking for an excuse to divorce his wife of six years. I gave him that means. I was the convenient catalyst.

Within a year after we had met, he literally bought himself a divorce, gained joint custody of his toddler daughter, and we got married. We exchanged vows aboard a lavish yacht amidst our families, close friends, some business associates, and his young child with whom I was becoming heartbreakingly close. Interestingly, her birthday was the exact day (but different year) of my daughter's death; loving and caring for her became the only parenting left to me. After our wedding, my husband and I threw ourselves into the best lifestyle southern California had to offer. Once again I felt secure in the bonds of a loving family—something I hadn't experienced in many years.

My husband loved his work. It was his first priority. (Eventually, it became his escape.) To him, leisure time meant that he was not being productive or useful. His economic success flourished, and his drive for money afforded us considerable flexibility, security, and luxury. As the years progressed, however, my husband and I became close friends rather than lovers, more platonic than passionate. We began moving in different directions, defined by our roles and responsibilities.

Four years into our marriage, my husband had an affair with a young, attractive divorcee with two young children. She worked and dealt with the same clients as my husband. One day, I came home unexpectedly and overheard him speaking with her on the phone. From the conversation, I knew immediately they were having an affair. Perhaps because of the close bond I had with my stepdaughter or because of the fateful way we met and fell in love, I never dreamed he would be unfaithful to me.

I confronted him immediately. When he realized I had heard him on the phone, he didn't even try to deny my accusations. I demanded a meeting with the two of them, threatening to leave him if he didn't comply. I wanted to know firsthand what she looked like, what her voice sounded like, how she dressed, how she carried herself. He picked up the phone and called her right in front of me and asked that she meet him at a local restaurant the next day. No doubt she thought it was just another rendezvous.

She arrived at the restaurant about ten minutes after my husband and I were seated. A young woman, in her late twenties, she was very pretty and composed (if she was shocked to see me sitting there, she didn't show it). She took a seat next to him, and, as they both faced me, the story unfolded. The two of them had met at a business function while I was in New York on a brief trip. She seemed to know everything there was to know about my marriage and me. I also learned that my husband had "entertained" her in our home while I had been away, and that they had been intimate without protection. She was quite clear and confident in her intentions—my husband was in love with her and was going to leave me.

I pointed out to her that a few weeks of sex did not equal love. I also pointed out that her idealized vision of marrying my husband didn't include the less-than-romantic realities that came along with it. She dug her heels in deeper and stood her ground, determined to win the battle for my husband. I was too angry, too hurt, and too disgusted with both of them to continue the meeting. I left the restaurant, driving off with a screech of tires.

A short time later, my husband returned home and begged my forgiveness. He claimed that I had become too busy, too detached, and that he had been lonely and vulnerable and needed a shoulder. (There was that typical response—he blamed *me* for his behavior!) In the months that followed, my husband claimed the affair was over. He frantically continued to shower me with flowers and more flowers and expensive gifts and speeches that begged my forgiveness. He had been through one very costly divorce already. Quite cynically, I felt certain that my husband would do anything he could to save our marriage·rather than split his wallet again. My time, meanwhile, was devoted primarily to my stepdaughter and ailing father-in-law.

As the months passed, however, I began to suspect they were seeing each other again. Little signs began cropping up here and there, so I confronted my husband. Unwillingly, he verified my suspicions. I decided it was time to have a therapy session involving the three of us. I wanted to bring things to a head in the presence of an impartial observer. Reluctantly, my husband and his lover agreed. During the session, the atmosphere in the room was tense, tearful, anxious, and hurtful as I listened to this woman tell the therapist how my husband didn't love me and wanted out of the marriage. "He doesn't love you, he doesn't want to be with you. He loves me, wants to be with me."

After I had heard enough, I very quietly said to my husband, "So go." A tense silence followed. The therapist looked at my husband and asked, "So who's it going to be? Your wife, your lover, or me? (Just kidding.)" My husband looked at both of us, then his lover stood up. I was sure they were going to leave together, but he looked at her and said, "I am not leaving with you. I love my wife and I am going to try and work it out." Whether he stayed out of fear, love, or guilt I don't know. What I do know is that my emotions were all mixed up and confused at that point. I told him flat out that he might as well leave with her because if I stayed with him it would be only out of love for his daughter and my financial security. The truth is I didn't feel the same way about him.

Like many women who have discovered their husbands have been unfaithful, I was devastated by the lack of respect my husband had shown me by sharing intimate details of our life with this woman. That intimacy caused more pain than the sexual relationship they shared.

This entire experience opened my eyes to some very important realities. People in love want to believe that what they hear from their lovers or cheating spouses is honest and true. A wife wants so much to believe her husband when he tells her his affair is over and the lover has meant nothing to him. At the same time, his lover is confident that he is being just as truthful when he claims she is number one in his life. *Everyone* wants to believe that the information spoken by the betraying spouse is accurate. In my case, my husband's lover sincerely believed that he loved her and was going to leave me. Yet, he didn't. We were both in love with the same man, and each of us felt as if we had the edge. We were both privy to secret information, but my husband's lover really never got the "full" picture of him. Sure, she knew what he was like at work and bonded with him through the details and stories he shared with her, but this was a mere snapshot in the photo album of his life. She never even considered that he might be unfaithful to her.

As discussed earlier in this book, millions of men and women enter affairs believing that they can handle them, manage them, and be immune from any fallout in the end. If you are flirting with the notion of having an affair, then you probably think this also. Think again! People don't have affairs without hurting others. Do you really believe that an affair will provide the pieces you believe are missing from your life? An affair is not a practical solution to anyone's problems, no matter what the circumstances. Matter of fact, in virtually every case, betrayal ends up only intensifying your problems. Your secure home, your finances, your emotional investment in your family, your children, your extended family, and everything else you hold dear is put in jeopardy.

Before getting involved in an affair, try to work backwards by starting with the consequences. Are you prepared to deal with the ramifications of getting caught? Are you willing to possibly lose your spouse, home, family, and good name, not to mention your financial security, house, car, and other assets? Be prepared to lose the respect of family, friends, and colleagues. Think of what it would be like to jeopardize your job. Your professional status. All of these things can happen. And they can happen to you.

## My Last and Final Affair

It began with friendship, as so many affairs do. He was a landscape designer my husband had hired to work on our property. A rugged individual, he had a magnetic personality that attracted others the moment he walked into a room. Easily the most charismatic man I had ever met, he was filled with positive energy, warmth, and confidence.

Almost immediately, we became fast friends. I learned that his past had been as checkered as mine—he had betrayed his wife a number of times. After several years of marriage, he claimed to have had a spiritual awakening. As a result, he formed a "contract" with God to be a loving, faithful spouse. He and his wife even renewed their wedding vows. He believed his newfound faith was strong enough to prevent him from straying again.

I couldn't deny that this man's spirit attracted me like a magnet. We began sharing long philosophical discussions about God and life and spirituality. Until then, religion had not been very important to me, yet I was fascinated by this man's faith, which he shared so easily. I somehow felt that all the tragedies in my life precluded a benevolent God. Over time, the intimacy we shared in these conversations became more threatening to our marriages than any sexual encounter could have been.

As my "spiritual" relationship with this man grew, my husband developed a close relationship with him as well. They were good friends and my husband trusted him enough to confide in him about me and the frustrations he was feeling in our marriage. You see, after my husband's affair, our marriage and the relationship between us changed. I no longer trusted him, nor did I want to have sex with him as he had had unprotected sex with his lover. I stayed in the marriage because it was comfortable and I loved his daughter and cared for his dad very much. Our lives had settled into a strained routine.

Soon the initial attraction I felt for my new friend escalated into a burning physical desire, and a few months after we met, we crossed over the boundary of friendship and became lovers. Somehow, my husband's confidences in this man added a thrill and excitement to our relationship before the affair began. And neither of us expected to fall in love, but we did. Eventually, we told our spouses.

Needless to say, our affair affected everyone in our lives— our spouses, the children, and our extended families and friends. Most of all, it affected the two of us, even to this day. My husband had no idea how to compete with this "ideal" man, and our lives became a series of confrontations, deceitful situations, and shattered dreams.

Eventually, I wanted to end this affair and salvage my marriage. My husband, however, had really had it and wasn't sure he still wanted to keep the marriage intact. He had become obsessed with my affair, and, possibly to retaliate, he had other relationships himself. He continually brought up my infidelity and couldn't seem to let it go. Eventually, the discord that had been created by our respective affairs wore him down and outweighed his desire to rebuild the marriage. In some ways, I suspect that the pain he was feeling had more to do with the betrayal of his friend, my lover, than it had to do with me. Eventually, the marriage ended in divorce.

## SUMMING IT UP

While the fact that I have played every role in the triangle may be unusual, many of the emotions and reactions I experienced in most of my affairs were very typical. I found myself reacting in much the same way other men and women do when they are affected by infidelity. Every affair has its own set of unique circumstances, but all acts of betrayal, no matter how peculiar the situation, are made up of similar feelings of pain and frustration. When it comes to unfaithfulness, suffering appears to be universal.

# 5 Relationship Dynamics

*"I told my wife the truth. I told her I was seeing a psychiatrist. Then she told me the truth—she was seeing a psychiatrist, two plumbers, and a bartender."*

—Rodney Dangerfield

As you saw in Chapter 4, the various roles that make up an affair are fraught with similarities. This chapter takes things a step further and describes the different combinations of people who actually make up an affair within the love triangle—either two married individuals or a married person and a single person. Same-sex relationships are also discussed. This chapter explores some of the characteristics specific to the different sets of lovers involved in an affair. Also discussed are some of their common problems and pitfalls.

## TWO MARRIED PEOPLE

Insofar as any affair runs smoothly, the triangle involving two married people is likely to run the smoothest. The fact that both parties are married forces each to be very careful—both have a lot at stake. They tend to be very understanding and accepting of the other's roles with respect to work, family, daily routines, children, and responsibilities within the respective marriages. Each shares similar inconveniences, obstacles, potential risks, and eventual consequences. In most cases, neither person really wants or expects a marital breakup; a romantic interlude is merely a diversion.

However, because *two* marriages and possibly two or more sets of children may be in jeopardy, the frustration the lovers experience in getting together is doubly difficult. *Both* parties must manufacture plausible excuses and reasons to slip away in order to rendezvous. And because married lovers typically have so much to risk between them, consequences of such an affair can be particularly devastating, especially if both want to keep their marriages, families, and financial security intact. The fear of the affair being discovered is something each one lives with constantly.

When married lovers are of the same sex, the sexuality issue further compounds the importance of the affair's secrecy. Being married, most same-sex lovers in the triangle want their sexual preferences kept under wraps. These lovers, whether two men or two women, share feelings that bear little resemblance to the ones they share with their spouses.

The fact that both parties are of the same sex, however, may actually make an affair easier to keep hidden. Most people do not see anything suspicious in two men or two women spending a great deal of time together. Even traveling and sharing a room won't cause most people to raise an eyebrow. People are more apt to be suspicious of married men and women who work or socialize together.

Affairs between two married people, whether they involve heterosexual or same-sex partners, usually terminate with the players going back to their respective spouses. Each have marriages on the line, and divorce can be messy and costly. These realities usually become crystal clear to those involved (even if it is only until the cycle repeats itself).

## A MARRIED PERSON AND A SINGLE PERSON

The majority of affairs occur between someone who is married and someone who is single. Unlike lovers who are each married, the dynamics of this combination make it even more difficult to keep an affair secret. Typically, the married half of this duo is more likely to have a greater number of pressures and responsibilities, such as a spouse, possibly children, and household matters to which he or she must attend. Such commitments add to the difficulty in "getting away" in order to keep the affair going. Single lovers, on the other hand, are usually less involved with family and other commitments, and they are able to have a lot more free time. They expect their married lovers to be with them during this time, regardless of how difficult it may be for them.

In a number of these triangles, single lovers (especially the "other" men) are not looking for long-term committed relationships. Getting together with those who are already married or involved fits comfortably into their agenda. To them, married lovers are "safe." They are not likely to make many demands on their single paramours. Most don't want to jeopardize their own marriages.

While this profile fits nicely into the plans of those who are not looking for any long-term bonds, most single lovers view the commitments of their married lovers as burdens. At some point during an affair, most will find themselves growing impatient with their partners. They will find themselves getting tired of waiting around for the magic moments that are spared them. Most of the time, there will come a point at which single lovers begin making demands or issuing ultimatums. It is at this point that many affairs die.

*An attractive woman in her late thirties, Diane's first love has always been playing the piano. Although she hasn't achieved fame as a concert pianist, she does play in public occasionally and gives private lessons, mostly to children. Her husband is a high-powered businessman who is totally immersed in a job that keeps him away from home most of the time. She loves her husband and has always tolerated his job because it allows her the wealthy lifestyle to which she*

has become accustomed. When Diane isn't giving piano lessons, she fills her days by playing tennis, raising funds for
her favorite charities, or working out at a local health spa.

Referring to herself as a "married single," Diane believed she was content with her life . . . that is, until she met
Bobby. The divorced father of one of her piano students,
Bobby had boyish good looks and magnetic charm. Diane's
immediate attraction to him left her a little confused and
feeling somewhat guilty. One night, Diane ran into Bobby
at the health spa. They started talking, and decided to continue their conversation over a couple of fruit smoothies in
the juice bar. Their chat was friendly and innocent, but for
the next few weeks, Diane couldn't get Bobby out of her
mind. Her heart leapt each time she saw him at the spa,
which became a regular Tuesday-night "thing." They found
their conversations becoming more and more personal.
Bobby talked about the intimate details of his divorce, while
Diane shared her feeling of loneliness due to her "absentee"
husband. Within a short time, they were no longer able to
deny their obvious attraction for each other, and the affair
began.

The relationship continued through the summer and
into the fall. Arranging to be together was fairly easy, as
Diane's husband wasn't around most of the time, but they
still had to be careful not to get caught. Diane quickly
became addicted to all of the attention Bobby provided, and
the sex was exciting and fulfilling. She really felt she had it
all—a husband who provided financial security and a lover
who satisfied her emotional and sexual needs. Bobby, on the
other hand, was falling in love with Diane. He soon grew
tired of having to see her on the sly and became possessive
and increasingly jealous of having to share her with her
husband. He wanted her all to himself.

Bobby began urging Diane to leave her husband, but she
wasn't about to make such a drastic move. She knew her husband was strong and powerful and didn't take kindly to "losing" in any aspect of his life. She feared what would happen

*if she tried to leave him; besides, she wasn't about to give up all the comforts that her marriage provided. All Diane wanted to do was maintain the affair, plain and simple.*

*Bobby didn't see things from Diane's point of view and began issuing ultimatums. He finally threatened to leave if she didn't take steps toward ending her marriage. Wanting the romance to continue, Diane kept putting Bobby off until he finally had had enough. Amidst her heartfelt protests, Bobby finally walked out on Diane and the affair.*

Like Bobby, many single lovers who have already gone through a divorce may encourage their married lovers to take the same action. They tend to offer advice on ways to end the marriage and give specific survival tips for getting through the divorce. For a spouse who is contemplating ending a marriage, this information can be helpful. If, however, like Diane, the married lover is not willing to leave his or her spouse, this advice will be viewed as unwelcomed pressure. In most affairs between a married and a single person, the married parties do not want a divorce. They intend to keep their marriages intact while maintaining relationships with their lovers. They want to have it all, but it just doesn't seem to happen, at least not for very long.

Then there are those situations in which at least one of the individuals involved in the affair has no genuine feelings for the other. The tryst is nothing more than a fling, a means to sexual satisfaction, or something to break up the boredom of everyday life. And while such a case may seem innocuous enough, the situation doesn't always pan out the way it was intended. Take the next story, for example.

*I was in my late thirties and had been married for about eight years. My wife was tops—kind, compassionate, and supportive. She was also a great cook and encouraged me to maintain my outside interests. We both had decent jobs (I was a local politician, and she was a middle school principal) and we lived quite comfortably. The problem? For me,* our marriage had started to get a little boring. The solution? I began having extramarital affairs—flings, really, mostly one-night stands. I liked the women I slept with, but never let myself get involved any further. After all, I wasn't looking to replace my wife, I was only trying to spice up my life a little.

One night, my wife and I attended a party at which I met this incredible woman. She was physically gorgeous, as well as warm and intelligent. Her shy, demure nature only added to her appeal. She was mesmerizing and I knew I had to have her. To my delight, she agreed to meet me the following night. Not only was she beautiful, I found her to be great in bed! I knew this was more than a one-night stand. I had to see her again.

I soon discovered that her sexual appetite was a voracious one, and I could barely keep up with her. At her insistence, we met several times a week. At first it was great, but then her demands began to get out of hand. I told her I had a problem seeing her so often, and I wanted to cool things a little. Unlike my other lovers, she protested vehemently, threatening to tell my wife everything. Against my will, I tried to appease her and continue the affair . . . but things had changed. I was so turned off to her that sex started to become a real struggle. The sight of her literally "shut down" all of my systems.

Infuriated, she marched to the local press and exposed our affair. Of course, I denied everything. She was unable to prove her accusations, but the story had done its damage. Doubt was cast on my reputation and I lost the next election. My wife wanted to believe me, but she couldn't help being suspicious. A disturbing silence pervades our marriage now, as the past hangs over our heads. I had no idea that what began as a simple, uncomplicated one-night stand could escalate into something so damaging.

The experience of this married man indicates, among other things, just how vulnerable a person is when he or she entrusts a lover with personal intimacies. Like it or not, the power a lover wields should not be denied or minimized.

What about same-sex relationships between marrieds and singles? As mentioned earlier, because society in general has difficulty dealing with issues of homosexuality, the discovery of this type of affair can be doubly destructive to both partners. One or both can be bisexual or homosexual, or the affair can be nothing more than an exercise to satisfy a person's sexual curiosity. No matter what, when a same-sex affair is exposed, the betrayed partner has other issues to deal with besides a cheating spouse.

> *Stephanie stopped by her fiancée's house one afternoon to pick up some books. She hadn't expected Sam to be home, but when she saw his car in the driveway she thought how nice it would be to surprise him. And surprise him she did, as she walked in on him having sex with another man. "He broke my heart in a million pieces," Stephanie recalled sadly. And she was further hurt because he was so callous toward what she was feeling. Instead, he worried only about how confused he was.*
>
> *At twenty-one, Stephanie has certainly felt the pain of betrayal, and on a number of levels. The fact that she caught Sam in a homosexual act didn't thrill her, but that in itself wasn't the greatest source of her pain. Of course, the infidelity factor certainly hurt, but what Stephanie found most painful was that if she hadn't walked in on Sam, he may never have owned up to his sexual preference—and he would have gone through with the marriage anyway.*

Married partners may feel the extra weight of having to keep both their infidelity as well as the sexual nature of this affair under wraps. In many cases, they have the most to lose. In many instances, single lovers already may have "come out," owning up to their sexuality in spite of society's close-minded views. Often, they will pressure their married lovers into admitting their homosexuality as well. Single lovers, generally, have more power than their married partners (who appear to have more at risk) in this type of relationship.

Because of the unusual and somewhat scandalous nature of this type of affair, those involved also may find they have very few friends or family members with whom they can share this confidence. Feelings of isolation only add to the pressure.

## SUMMING IT UP

Whether you are in the beginning, middle, or at the end of an affair, no doubt you have been able to recognize yourself in this chapter. And if you are flirting with the idea of entering into such a relationship, this chapter has given you fair warning that the experience is not likely to be all hearts and roses. It is more apt to be a bouquet of thistles and thorns!

# 6 Through the Eyes of a Child

*"Children need models rather than critics."*

—Joseph Joubert
1842

*I* was a sophomore in college when my mom confided in me that she was having an affair. Her news came as a total shock. It was bad enough that my mother had made such a choice, but to burden me with it in this secretive fashion tormented me. Why did I have to be the confidante to her escapades? It's not as if she was sorry or felt guilty about the affair—she was thrilled with it. She wasn't concerned about her relationship with my father or the possible consequences of her actions. No. She was acting more like a mischievous child or a giddy schoolgirl who simply had to share her secret behavior with a friend. Well, I'm not her friend, I'm her daughter, and she placed me in a no-win situation.

I felt true sadness every time I looked at my dad. I feared his heart would break if he ever found out. My mother had sworn me to secrecy, and I kept her secret (I doubt if I could have told my dad about it anyway), but it was at the expense of my own peace of mind. I lived in a constant state of inner turmoil. I wondered how long my mom was going to continue the charade, and I also wondered how many other

*men she'd been with. The only thing I know for sure is that*
*I wish my mother hadn't put me in this impossible position.*

Children, no matter what their age, are typically the hidden casualties in betrayal. They are the ones who suffer in silence and feel the impact long after the adults have moved on. With all of the upheaval that surrounds infidelity and marital breakups, the kids are often the last to be noticed, the last ones whose feelings are acknowledged. And with such an increase in blended and extended families these days, it's no wonder that so many children who witness the breakup of their parents feel doubly threatened.

*After his parents' divorce when he was three, David had*
*little contact with his "real" mother. When David was four,*
*his dad married a woman named Danielle. Over the years,*
*David developed a warm, close relationship with Danielle,*
*who loved and treated him as if he were her own son. When*
*David was in his early teens, he noticed that Danielle had*
*started to become increasingly irritable, short-tempered, and*
*distant with both David and his dad. He mentioned this to*
*his friend Matt, who matter-of-factly told him that his father*
*was probably having an affair. That's what had happened to*
*Matt's parents before they divorced a few years earlier.*

*This troubled David, who began to suspect his father of*
*infidelity, even though he had no proof. Ironically, about a*
*year later it was Danielle who confessed that she was the*
*one who had been having an affair. Tearfully, she assured*
*both of them that the affair was over, and begged them both*
*to forgive her, but the family's foundation had been badly*
*shaken.*

*David's father, always a quiet man, became even quieter,*
*more withdrawn, which concerned David. And although*
*Danielle tried to re-establish the closeness she once had with*
*David, he found it hard to look her in the eyes. The trust*
*was gone. He looked at her as the second mother who had*
*betrayed him, and this weighed him down with great sad-*

*ness. Eventually, this sadness turned to anger. Once an honor student, David found it difficult to concentrate and his grades began to suffer. He started hanging around with a "drinking" crowd at school. He believed the alcohol helped dull his pain. The worst part was that his dad and Danielle were so busy dealing with their own pain, they didn't notice David's distress. He felt brokenhearted and totally alone.*

Children, especially teenagers, often have difficulty when it comes to verbalizing their feelings. They don't have a hard time asking for things that they want, such as a bigger allowance, a new computer, or more space, but they usually have enormous difficulty articulating things that bother them. Children caught up in their parent's extramarital affair generally have such mixed feelings that it may be almost impossible to process them. There are some kids who may be able to identify their feelings, knowing that the conflict between their parents has made them feel stressed out, nervous, and uncertain; but, they may fear that verbalizing these feelings will only add to the general tension in the house and actually could make things worse. So they choose to keep their feelings bottled inside, letting them brew. Commonly, this inner turmoil manifests itself in behavioral problems that range from drug and/or alcohol use, to disciplinary problems, to lack of interest in activities that they once enjoyed.

Watch for the following signs, which can be indicative of an older child or teenager who is troubled:

- *Poor grades and schoolwork.* Displays an inability to concentrate in school; suddenly has little interest in getting good grades.

- *Little or no initiative.* Seems withdrawn and no longer cares for hobbies, sports, or other subjects of former interest.

- *Changes in friendships.* Suddenly switches to a new crowd of friends.

- *Displays of extreme emotions.* A normally quiet, meek child may become wild and aggressive. Conversely, a child who is outgoing and assertive may become sullen and withdrawn.

- *Defiant.* Suddenly begins pushing limits—won't do chores; defies parents, teachers, or other authority figures; refuses to adhere to curfews or other rules.

- *Secretive.* Begins shutting out people; refuses to engage in conversations or share information about things they do or places they go.

In addition, adolescents may display changes in personal hygiene and show signs of all-around sloppiness. For example, they may "forget" to shower daily or stop wearing clean clothes. They may lose or gain startling amounts of weight. Suddenly, a child who is always easy to deal with may become a "problem," fighting with parents or teachers on any and every issue. Sleeping patterns may change as well. Some teenagers spend most of the day sleeping, while others find it difficult to sleep at all. Still others find themselves sleeping in odd shifts—staying up all night and sleeping during the day.

A young child who is troubled may exhibit signs that are more subtle than those of an adolescent, but don't overlook them. Keep your eye out for the following behaviors, which commonly signal a troubled young child:

- *Regression.* Shows signs of reverting to an earlier developmental stage—may begin talking "baby talk" or start sucking his or her thumb.

- *Sleep disturbances.* Has trouble sleeping or suddenly begins having bad dreams or nightmares (night terrors) with regularity.

- *Change of bladder and/or bowel control.* Suddenly begins wetting the bed.

- *Change in eating habits.* Has little or no appetite or wants to eat all of the time.

- *Emotional outbursts.* May begin crying, throwing temper tantrums, or displaying other forms of anger and aggression (often for no apparent reason).

- *Signs of insecurity.* Begins clinging to a parent or parents, not wanting them out of sight.

- *Lack of communication.* Becomes withdrawn and nonverbal.

Remember, no matter what their age, children can find themselves troubled over change or discord within the family unit. Your obligation and responsibility as a parent is to pay attention to these feelings; don't sweep them under the rug. Help your child feel secure amidst the turmoil.

## ON SHAKY GROUND

One of the most difficult things for children to deal with when they fear lack of harmony between their parents is not knowing where to turn for comfort or help. Parents, formerly the bedrock of the family and the solid base on which a child could always rely, are suddenly showing signs of instability. Depending on the situation and the personalities of the people involved, children are sometimes told either too much or too little about what's going on. Either way, the kids find themselves on shaky ground, not knowing whether or not the family will survive. They fear for their own futures, and often rightfully so. Take the following story, for example.

*Kim was the youngest of three children, and the only daughter. She had an upbeat personality, was popular with her peers, and an excellent student. Kim was very close to her father, although his job kept him away on business trips much of the time. In spite of the fact that her parents bickered a fair amount—mostly over money and the amount of* time her dad spent away from home—the family was close. Kim's older brothers worked at odd jobs during high school to help pay for life's necessary extras, like concert tickets and car insurance. Their father, who had had to do the same when he was young, didn't believe in large allowances or overindulging his children. Education, however, was a priority, and money had been put aside for college tuition.

Over time, the bickering between Kim's parents escalated into heated arguments that resulted in increasing numbers of serious fights. When Kim was in her senior year in high school, her dad confessed that he had been having an affair with a woman from his office for a number of years. All of those long weekends away from home weren't about business after all. The family was heartbroken when they learned of his affair, and nearly fell apart when he left them to move into a new house with his lover.

Suddenly the family's financial situation became more precarious than ever before. Kim's mother could barely keep up with the bills and mortgage, not to mention the mounting legal fees from the divorce. Worst of all, she was forced to use the money that had been set aside for Kim's college tuition.

The irony of the situation was that Kim's father was leading a lavish lifestyle. He bought a new house and a new boat; and he spared no expense in showering his lover with expensive jewelry and vacations. So what about Daddy's little girl? Kim felt betrayed and lost. She had to put her plans for college and a teaching career on hold, and she took a job instead. It was difficult for Kim to watch all of her friends leave for college the following September, but somehow, with the support of her mom and brothers, she got through it. The following year, she was granted a need-based scholarship at a local community college. Although it wasn't the school of her choice, she was happy to be going to college at all.

No doubt this feeling of betrayal will follow Kim and children like her for a long time, affecting their relationships, friendships, self-esteem, and self-confidence. Being a child or a teen is confusing enough. To be sent a signal that you don't matter, that one (or both) of your parents cares more about a lover than they care about you is devastating. If the child's living arrangement changes or the family's financial situation becomes strained, he or she may be forced to re-evaluate personal goals, dreams, and future plans, like Kim did in the story above. And don't minimize the fact that children tend to lose respect for parents who have been caught lying, cheating, and doing things they've always been told are wrong. Dealing with such a conflict can be enormously difficult for kids; it can subtly alter the course of a child's life.

Everyone needs time and space to adapt to change. It's vitally important that parents who are caught in the web of infidelity maintain an atmosphere in which their kids can approach them. Parents must be consistent, respectful, and they must *listen* to their children. These are real people in tiny bodies. Most important, parents must assure their children that they are in no way responsible for the family turmoil.

Outside counseling often works well during such times of family unrest, but timing is important. Many of the teenagers I've spoken to claim that at the onset of the family discord, they felt withdrawn and silent, and they didn't want to talk to anyone. Once things began to settle down, however, they were more inclined to verbalize their feelings and found counseling to be a great benefit. Other teens felt great comfort in professional counseling early on. As a caring parent, you must be sensitive to the approach that best suits your child's individual personality. Another important point—as a parent, you cannot expect your child to adjust to any stressful situation quickly, especially one that involves a traumatic family shakeup. Give your child the time he or she needs to come to terms with the situation. You must be a patient and loving figure throughout the adjustment period.

I encourage older children and teens to keep a journal and write down their feelings, their fears, their pain. This can be a very effective outlet in preventing them from keeping their problems bottled up inside. (By the way, journal writing works for adults, too!)

## MORE RAMIFICATIONS

Family problems often translate into missed holidays, birthdays, and other events that are especially important for children. Even though some kids, teens in particular, may complain about having to spend time with family, deep down they expect, want, and need this connection to those they love. Many kids who experience dysfunction within their own family units will gravitate toward their friends' families in an effort to regain the sense of closeness they crave. Other kids may become aggressive or even violent in order to vent their anger and frustration.

It is also common for some children to deny that anything is wrong with their parents' relationship, even when they have been made aware of the adultery issue. This person, after all, is someone who has been there for them for as long as they can remember—someone they have trusted, loved, admired, and turned to in times of need. It's not easy for any of us to realize that our heroes have feet of clay. For a child to realize that a parent is not perfect can be a huge blow. Even worse, in many cases of affairs and divorce, some parents place their children in the middle and use them as pawns. The following scenario is all too familiar:

> *Bill and Lydia had a storybook marriage and three beautiful children together. After a number of years, however, Lydia discovered Bill was having an affair. She immediately filed for divorce. Within a year, Bill remarried, although not to the woman who had been his lover. Throughout the divorce and afterwards, Bill and Lydia used the children as spies, informants, and shoulders to cry on. They told the children horrible things about each other. The kids were under constant pressure to take sides.*

Most children want to keep a connection with the cheating parent, even if it's a poor one. Pressuring a child to take sides and alienate the other parent is an unfair expectation. Not only is it difficult for most children to do, it can have psychologically damaging effects. Take the following story:

> *Susan and Jack had been married for twelve years and had two children. Jack's infidelity caused the marriage to end in a nasty divorce. Susan had great difficulty dealing with her anger and bitterness. When the children saw Jack on their weekend visits, she gave them orders to find out everything they could about their dad, especially if he was seeing anyone socially.*
>
> *Jack noticed that the kids always seemed stressed and nervous when they visited. Eventually, they told him about their mother's instructions, which had been upsetting them. Jack immediately confronted Susan and told her to back off. His life was none of her business and dragging the children into her "investigation" was horribly unfair to them. Susan was furious with the children for telling their father and she punished them immediately. This caused the children to clam up and start to withdraw from both parents.*
>
> *Within a short time, Susan began dating again. She left the children with sitter after sitter so she was free to socialize. They were constantly confused and frightened; they felt alone and abandoned.*

Some parents get so caught up in their affairs that they view their children as obstacles—roadblocks that stand in the way of time spent with lovers. Such resentment is clearly felt by the children, who have absolutely no idea why they've suddenly become a source of irritation and frustration. This leaves them standing alone on the sidelines, emotionally isolated.

When a marriage ends as the result of an affair, the cheating parent's lover is not likely to be a popular choice with the children. As a result, the parent may choose to keep them apart as much as possible. Often, this means spending less time with the children as they choose to be with their lovers instead.

> *Mary and Kevin's thirteen-year marriage ended when Mary left Kevin for Steven. Their children—seven-year-old Stacey and nine-year-old Chad—continued living with their dad.*
>
> *Whenever the children were around Steven, tension filled the air. Steven never particularly liked kids. He felt uncomfortable around Stacy and Chad, and made no attempt to hide his jealousy and resentment toward them and their relationship with Mary. He was constantly making nasty remarks to them and never missed an opportunity to belittle them.*
>
> *The children disliked Steven immensely and told their mother not bring him along on their visits with her. Mary agreed, but, predictably, she simply began coming around to see the kids less and less. In essence, she chose her relationship with Steven over the ones with her children.*

A very special, unique bond ties a parent to a child. Why is it then that infidelity can break that bond so easily, allowing parents to forget the responsibility they have to their kids? A parent who makes an obvious choice to be with a lover rather than his or her children, causes tremendous damage to a child's fragile ego. Although they may not realize it initially, children eventually get the message that they are not as important as they always thought they were. Such bruised feelings of self-worth can create deep-seated problems, immense emotional damage in children of any age.

## THE TV GENERATION

Today's youth grow up in front of the television, watching sophisticated adult shows and sitcoms in which adult themes are dealt with on a continued basis. Violence, betrayal, infidelity, love, sex, addiction—such themes are aired regularly

and played out for dramatic effect. Rarely, if ever, are any consequences of these themes shown. If, for instance, a character
gets shot in the shoulder, he doesn't exhibit the pain and life-
long hand movement problems such a wound would cause in
real life. Quite the contrary, he's up and at 'em an hour later.
When infidelity is the theme of a show or movie, typically it is
used only to intensify the high drama of the story line. Its very
real, far-reaching consequences are rarely spotlighted.

Children watch these shows day in and day out and start
to believe that behaviors such as adultery are a normal, ordinary part of everyday life. They don't realize just how difficult and complicated the ramifications can be—until, that is,
such behavior touches them personally. Until then, they don't
have an inkling of the real-life consequences.

Years of such exposure cause kids to mature quickly.
Because they sometimes talk and dress like mini-adults, we
sometimes forget that they are just kids, no matter how
adult-like they appear. These days, kids are well-versed on
subjects such as global warming, the deterioration of the
ozone layer, and the threat of nuclear war; they know all
about disk drives and Pentium chips; and they are well
aware of such "adult" subjects as homosexuality and sexually transmitted diseases. It's easy to forget they're just *kids*
no matter how broad their vocabularies or how sophisticated they may sound.

## THEY'RE STILL JUST KIDS

By the way, don't underestimate kids. They often realize that
something is amiss long before their parents think they know.
Children have almost a sixth sense when it comes to unspoken
tension. Parents may think their children are fast asleep and
can't hear them arguing in the middle of the night. Don't count
on it. Ever hear the expression, "the walls have ears"? They pick
up on more signs than most adults give them credit for. They
may hear a parent's hushed, secretive telephone conversation,
then watch it end abruptly when they walk into the room.

Children also may notice that one parent is away from home much more than usual, or that someone keeps hanging up whenever they answer the phone. They can't help but note how tempers seem constantly frayed, and how suddenly there seems to be less time for family activities. Out of guilt, some parents will give into their children's demands more easily than ever before. Others may not seem to care as much as they used to about their children's interests. For instance, their presence at little league games or tennis matches may become less frequent. Suddenly, mom or dad may allow their child to spend inordinate amounts of time at a friend's house, or they lift their teenager's curfew, allowing him or her to stay out until all hours. Oh yes, children certainly can sense when things are not "right."

And don't underestimate the magnitude of a child's emotional reactions to a rocky family situation. Any dramatic change or traumatic situation can be pretty scary, particularly for young children. They find it especially difficult to cope with such changes because they have no sense of history. The here and now is all that children, especially younger ones, comprehend. Typically, they have no idea that things eventually will get better. Imagine how scary that is. They don't realize that with time their pain will ease, problems will fade, and wounds will heal. For them, there is no end in sight for confusing, painful events like death and divorce, which seem to go on forever.

Adults, on the other hand, do know that time is a great healer. Through years of life experiences, they've learned that they *will* feel better, that eventually things *will* right themselves. After all, most adults have found themselves facing difficult situations and have learned first-hand that at some point the difficulty will pass. Children lack this sense of time and experience. They need to be told, reassured, and comforted. Yet all too often when infidelity strikes a family the adult members are so caught up in their own feelings and personal agendas that they forget about their children, who are often abandoned on the sidelines of the triangle.

## WHAT SHOULD PARENTS DO?

Many parents who are caught up in the throes of an affair fall into one of two camps. Some tend to dismiss the needs of their children, demoting them to second-string players behind their lovers. This can be most devastating to children, who cannot help but feel threatened and abandoned. Other parents overindulge their children to compensate for their own guilt. Smothering children with gifts and attention is less damaging than abandoning them, but in the long run, this can have negative ramifications as well. It's as if a parent is buying a child off. What kids need most is love, honesty, and understanding from a parent.

As a parent, what can you do to help your children deal with family turmoil? First, be open and honest with them and explain the situation as best you can. Details are not necessary, but honesty is. Reassure them that they are not responsible in any way for the conflict, and that you love them and will always do what is best for them. When my last marriage ended, I left my stepdaughter even though I loved her to distraction. Things were already hard enough for her having a mother *and* a stepmother *and* a new woman in her dad's life. I didn't want her to feel torn even further between her father's new love interest and me. If I thought she would have benefitted by my staying in California, I would have, but I could see that as a budding teenager she was already stuck in the middle of far too many problems. I felt it would be better for her if I made a clean break and let her father be the guiding force in her life. To this day, I have kept his affair hidden from her, although she knew about mine.

For our children's sake, we must answer their questions. Again, they don't necessarily need all of the details, but they do need to face the reality that parents are not perfect; they make mistakes. Children must also know that their parents intend to learn from their mistakes. Especially during turbulent times, children need to feel respected and loved. As a parent, it's important that you are aware of this and try to fulfill their needs. All too often, parents don't address their children's feelings because they don't know how. At the very least, do not make things more difficult than they are already. When dealing with your children, specifically, do not:

- Pressure them to take sides.

- Ask them to spy for you.

- Expect them to fill the void that the loss of a lover or spouse will create.

- Overload them with details (but be honest about changes that will affect them).

- Minimize their reactions and emotions.

- Allow guilt to control good parenting sense.

- Deny your own negative feelings in a misguided attempt to "spare" their feelings.

- Emphasize negative feelings over hopeful ones.

In addition, it is important to assure your children that this unsettling period in their lives is temporary. It *will* pass. Assure them that time will eventually ease their fears, sadness, and anxiety. And be sympathetic. Let them know you understand how difficult this transition is, and that you will always be there to support and help them through it. They will learn and grow stronger from it. It is what recovery and change are all about.

## INDIVIDUAL DIFFERENCES

Children are people, and all people are different. Each has his or her own coping skills. Some are better able to deal with painful truths than others. Age is an important consideration. Younger children, especially, will find it difficult to understand what is going on. Sharing only the most basic information is generally the most appropriate way to deal with them.

Older children, especially teens, can be quite savvy and

are not easily fooled. They should be told the truth, but it isn't necessary to share all of the intimate details surrounding the affair. Too much information can be damaging, while too little can seem like dishonesty. When they discover a parent's infidelity, teens commonly react with embarrassment. They are often too ashamed to share this personal information with their friends, and may begin withdrawing from others socially. This isolation only adds to their burden.

Younger children commonly react by believing their parents' marital breakdown is somehow their fault. It is vitally important that they be reassured and told that they are not to blame. It is certainly not their fault, and they do not have the power to fix the situation either.

Some children try to "replace" the parent who has left the family, taking on responsibilities that they should never be allowed to take on. A daughter may try to assume the role of an absent mother and feel it is up to her to take care of the family chores that her mother once did. A son may feel that he must become the "man of the house" in lieu of an absent father. But children are not caretakers, and it is *never* a child's place to take on the pressure of such roles. Of course, kids can take on age-appropriate responsibilities to pitch in and help preserve the family unit, but they must not feel the burden of a parental role.

This is also a time for open discussions on issues surrounding infidelity and divorce, especially with older children. Intimacy, sex, romance, and commitment are issues that should be dealt with to prevent a child's own future relationships from becoming negatively affected. In many cases, counseling can be extremely helpful at this time.

## SETTING AN EXAMPLE

As we all know, behavioral patterns tend to repeat themselves. Generally speaking, children are inclined to mimic the actions they witness. For instance, if a child grows up among family members who typically curse and swear, there's a good chance that he or she will eventually exhibit the same behavior. Many children of alcoholics and drug users become substance abusers themselves. And children of promiscuous parents may display similar behavior. Some become sexually immoral or unfaithful to their partners, while others may fear sex and become inhibited and frigid. Either way, unless issues surrounding their parents' behavior are resolved, children can find it difficult to develop normal, healthy, loving relationships.

## SUMMING IT UP

I truly believe that as a society we tend to shortchange our children. We spend billions of dollars on things like diets, fountain-of-youth cosmetics, and health club memberships to preserve our appearances. We shower ourselves with the latest toys and gadgets, and we go to great lengths to keep ourselves entertained. When it comes to our children, we also want the best—good educations, fashionable clothing, vacations, and lots of friends. Unfortunately, in our efforts to attain these priorities, we sometimes lose sight of fulfilling our children's greatest needs. We forget to talk to them, spend time with them, give them the emotional and intellectual tools they'll need in their adult lives. We want them to develop values and morals, yet we don't always serve as good examples—we either forget, deny, or don't care about the ramifications and consequences of our actions. We may talk ourselves into believing that our behavior won't affect our children, but it will.

Children typically idealize their parents and their family life. When the reality of an affair sets in, these views become tarnished. Pride and anger may prevent children from communicating with their parents, but it is the responsibility of the parents to keep the lines of communication open with their kids. Most important, they must ensure their children that they are loved, the situation is not their fault, and that, as parents, they will always be there for them.

# PART THREE

# Prevention, Intervention, and Recovery

# 7 Facing Reality

*"I've only slept with men I've been*
*married to. How many women can*
*make that claim?"*

—Elizabeth Taylor

ow often do you rummage through your closet in
search of the right costume, the right mask to wear as
part of your daily façade? Most of us do, and to a certain degree this is considered expected and a natural part of
our daily routine. We go out of our way to reveal only those
aspects of ourselves that we want others to know and only at
specific times.

If you are involved in an affair, however, you will quickly
discover that in order to maintain this deception, you will
need to juggle a number of different masks—layers of them.
You'll wear one when you lie to your spouse and another
when you deceive your children. Your lover will see you in
one mask, while your friends, family members, colleagues,
and other individuals you encounter will view you in another. And of course, don't forget about the most destructive
mask of all—the one you wear when you lie to yourself. As
an affair escalates, so will the lying and deception, layers
upon layers of false faces. As the masks pile up and often
need to be switched at a moment's notice, you'll find this

masquerade becoming all-consuming—a way of life. And these masks will cloud your ability to know yourself, to see who you really are, naked and void of the masquerade.

Most extramarital affairs require a great deal of energy. After all, maintaining them takes a lot of effort. You have to arrange and adjust these masks to fit your schedule to steal time for those clandestine meetings. You must also make up as well as keep track of all the lies and deception that follow. Eventually, like most affairs, yours will probably be discovered, and the masks you have tried so hard to conceal will be revealed for all to see.

Facing the reality of infidelity involves stripping away the masks you have constructed as you uncover to re-cover the real you. It's about accountability—answering to yourself and to those you love. Understanding this concept and taking responsibility for your actions will help you unravel the fantasies and see the affair and your role in it for what it really is, not for what you pretend it to be. It means staying loyal to those close to you, those who deserve and expect your integrity and honesty. Accountability forces truthfulness and ownership of your actions—concepts that do not go hand in hand with infidelity.

Love and happiness may be intertwined, but an affair is not the way to achieve this over the long haul. Typically, affairs are born to fill a void or satisfy a need. They may be entered into to add excitement or break the boredom of one's life, to overcome loneliness, to recapture a feeling of lost romance, or to achieve sexual satisfaction. A person may consider an affair as a means of revenge—to get back at a cheating partner or to gain power within a relationship. This type of relationship may seem like the best way to fill such needs; but, in reality, infidelity is a poor option for resolving any life conflict. In most instances, it serves only to create new ones. The surest way to avoid the problems that infidelity invariably brings is to refrain from having this type of relationship in the first place. Affairs can best be prevented if you first take an honest look at their consequences.

## 20/20 FORESIGHT

*In Greek mythology, Cassandra was the daughter of Priam, King of Troy. Apollo, the God of Light and Healing, loved Cassandra and gave her the gift of foresight, the ability to see into the future. When Cassandra spurned his love, Apollo was angered and resented having given her such a powerful gift. To this end, he decided to render her power meaningless by deeming that no one ever believe a word she said. According to the myth, Cassandra tried to warn the people of Troy of the impending peril of the Trojan horse—a "gift" of the Greeks. Her warnings went unheeded, however, and Troy was ultimately destroyed.*

Unfortunately, once you are standing amidst the disastrous and often far-reaching ramifications of an extramarital affair, it's usually too late to stop the dominoes of destruction from cascading around you. If only you had considered, had understood the ramifications of infidelity before taking that first step. If only you had taken the time to take an honest look at the possible consequences of such actions when you were just flirting with the idea of having an affair, just entertaining the fantasy of having a lover, you could have saved yourself untold grief and upheaval.

But much like the warnings of Cassandra, even the most direct, sincerest advice will not deter some people from having an affair if they really want to. It's human nature to seek the most gratifying, immediate solution for any problem, and for some people, an affair may seem like just the answer. Easy? Maybe. Without consequences? No way! Unfortunately, when on the verge of an affair, considering the consequences is often difficult because the heart—not the mind—is usually leading the way. If you are like most people, you probably think you can handle it, that you can somehow escape the financial, social, emotional, familial, and potentially legal ramifications of adultery. You believe the risks involved (and there are many) apply to other people, not you. Undoubtedly, you think your situation is different, special. *You're* special. You can beat the odds. But you won't.

## STARS IN YOUR EYES

Realize that an affair is more about fantasy than it is about fact. If you are bound by a committed relationship, you may look at your lover (or potential lover) and see everything that you feel your own partner lacks. If you are single and involved with a married man or woman, you may view your lover as someone who is unlike anyone you've ever known before. With stars in your eyes and magic in your heart, you believe this new person is your soul mate. He or she is kinder, gentler, more understanding than anyone on earth, especially in the beginning of the relationship, and certainly when compared with your spouse. With time, however, as the relationship goes beyond the stage of blind passion, the inevitable flaws will start to surface. "Why didn't I see those chinks in the armor from the start?" The answer is simple—you weren't looking for them.

Leading with emotions, with hearts instead of minds, most people get so caught up in the fantasy of an affair that they refuse to consider the harsh realities. Romance is a distorter of reality, which is why it can be easy to fall in love. Staying in love is another matter. If you really *saw* and *knew* the person, it would be a lot more difficult to fall in love.

If you have never had an affair, consider yourself blessed. The outcomes of infidelity are just too expensive. They run a high cost in wasted lives, spent emotions, and cold hard cash. If you are dreaming about that ideal lover and fantasizing about the excitement and pleasures you think an affair might bring to your life, take off those rose-colored glasses and view the affair realistically. Don't allow your idealizing to push you into a course of action that you will invariably regret later.

## SHARE THE FANTASY WITH EYES WIDE OPEN

To help open your eyes to the stark realities of an affair *before* actually taking that first step, force yourself to do something even more adventurous first. Share your fantasies of an anticipated affair with someone you trust. This simple intervention alone can help you see more clearly just how major this step is. Bringing your visions into the open will help cast the light of reality on them. You can view the situation more honestly and anticipate the outcome more clearly. The simple act of sharing your secret may actually rob it of some of its mystery and excitement, allowing you to see the pitfalls and ramifications better, rather than the gratifications you expect.

If you are not willing to share your fantasies of having an affair with another person, at least engage in a mental exercise yourself. Step by step, envision yourself with the ideal lover you've chosen. Think of all the positives. Your new lover is warm, caring, generous, and attentive. He or she fulfills your deepest desires and needs. Imagine the two of you in a romantic setting—maybe a candlelit dinner for two in front of a roaring fireplace, or a walk on a starlit beach with a bottle of chilled champagne. As you continue the fantasy, keep the rose-colored glasses on . . . no jangling of telephones or children to disturb the mood. Dim lights. Soft music. It's every Hollywood romance brought to life just for you. Your lover looks at you with passion and desire. Close your eyes and bask in the dream.

Now open your eyes and carefully remove the glasses. Begin to see the details, the lies, the deception. Notice the scheduling difficulties in keeping your dream scenario going. Hand in hand, you walk with your lover down the hotel corridor to your room—but who sees you? A cousin who's at the hotel attending a conference? A neighbor who is checking out the main ballroom for her daughter's up-and-coming wedding? When your partner discovers the napkin or matches with the hotel logo in your coat pocket, how will you explain it? How many times will you have to skip your son's soccer games or your daughter's piano recitals to meet your lover? How long will you continue to break promises to your loved ones without hurting them, upsetting them, arousing their suspicions? What happens if you are exposed to a sexually transmitted disease? How will you explain that to your spouse, your doctor, your friends? What happens when your lover begins demanding more of the relationship than you are willing to give, and the romantic interlude transforms into destructive obsession? What if your spouse (or lover) sues for alienation of affection? Imagine the drawn-out court battle, the embarrassing details, the expense, the shame. Don't exclude these ugly details as your fantasy unfolds.

What lies must you tell to keep your affair hidden? What risks—professional, personal, financial—will you be running? Do you *really* think you can keep such a secret? Can you resist confiding in someone? What about your lover? Can he or she keep from sharing the relationship with a close friend or two or three or . . .? What happens when the affair is finally blown wide open? Are you prepared to face the anger, the disappointment, the rejection? Don't think for one minute that your secret will be kept. It won't. And it will likely be uncovered when you least expect it.

Imagine the look on your mate's face when he or she hears the news of your betrayal. Are there children involved? Consider their reactions, their shock, their shame. What would it feel like to lose all that you value? Are you *really* willing to start over with nothing more than your lover? And, by the way, do you honestly think he or she will accept you with nothing but the shirt on your back? How much of this relationship is based on external romantic trappings versus reality?

Without the rose-colored glasses, the picture of your affair isn't quite as "rosy," is it? This is why it is so important to start at the end, by considering the consequences. Remember, odds are that you will get caught and you will lose all that you value. Don't delude yourself into believing that an affair will make you a more compatible spouse, either. What you *should* understand is that your marriage (or partnership) is far more likely to end in divorce than it will be improved or strengthened. You owe it to yourself and to those around you to really focus on the consequences of your actions before you go past the point of no return.

*Suzanne was the "other woman." Unlike most players who occupy this side of the triangle, she actually married the man she'd had the affair with; but even then, her fantasy didn't turn out the way she had expected.*

*"I was with Robert for five years before he divorced his wife. The executive of a very large corporation, he could afford to keep me on the side. He provided everything—a beautiful condo, nice clothes, wonderful trips—just about everything I wanted. The one thing he wasn't able to give me, however, was himself.*

*Because of his wife and family, I had to settle for random snippets of time whenever he could spare them. At first, I was grateful for the stolen moments, but soon, I grew tired of being alone so much of the time. I spent holidays alone and attended weddings and parties unescorted. It didn't take long before I began pressuring Robert to leave his wife, and eventually he did. His marriage ended in a bitter divorce and he lost custody of his children. But I didn't care. My only concern was that he was free.*

*My fantasy became complete when Robert and I married. We were able to be together—no more feelings of guilt, no more lonely nights. After a couple years of happiness, things began to change. Robert started showing signs of boredom in our marriage and with me. Given his past history, I began to suspect him of seeing someone else. All of the signs were there—phone calls in the middle of the night (which Robert took in another room), his sudden interest in getting into better shape, and an increase in the number of 'weekend' business trips. Although he laughed at my accusations at first, calling me paranoid, eventually he admitted* the truth. He said he had begun feeling bored with me and tried to alleviate this boredom with the excitement of another woman.

Looking back on it now, I don't know why I thought I could trust him to be faithful. After all, I was the primary witness to his infidelity during his first marriage. His behavior repeated itself!"

The secret of an affair usually will not last a lifetime. Take the following story of one man's experience that was shared in one of my support groups.

Mike was married to Kitty. He was in love with her and happy with his marriage, but he couldn't deny his attraction to Joanne, one of his colleagues. After a little "harmless" flirting, Mike found himself unable to resist Joanne's advances. Like most people who have taken that first step into the world of adultery, Mike believed he could have it all—a marriage as well as a mistress. He was a smart guy, after all, and felt secure that he could keep the secret.

One night, shortly after the affair had begun, Mike and his wife were making love. Consumed with thoughts of Joanne and their heated lunchtime tryst that day, Mike accidentally whispered Joanne's name in Kitty's ear. He hadn't even realized what he said until he felt Kitty's warm embrace immediately turn stone cold as she asked, "And just who is Joanne?" In shock himself, Mike was at a loss for words. His attempt to explain only made him look guilty—like a kid who got caught with his hand in the cookie jar. The damage was done.

For the next several weeks, Kitty was relentless in her quest to discover "Joanne." Mike simply kept denying knowing anyone with that name. He boldly told Kitty that the only Joanne he knew was the one who worked in his office, and she was engaged. He even allowed himself to get angry at his wife's accusations. Although she remained somewhat suspicious for a while, Kitty eventually let it go.

*Mike, in the meantime, quickly ended his affair. He had learned just how easy it was to get caught. He knew he had put his marriage on the line. He reassessed his relationship with Kitty. He knew he loved her and realized just how empty his life would be without her. He looked back at his liaison with Joanne and saw it for what it really was—a sexual diversion, a fling. It certainly wasn't worth losing his wife over.*

Mike knew he was one of the few lucky ones. He was given a second chance to preserve his marriage in spite of his illicit relationship.

## BUILD ON YOUR MARRIAGE

Most marriages and other monogamous long-term relationships come about because two people love each other. They are attracted to and appear bonded to one another. Something special about their union creates good chemistry, positive feelings. Together they are more than the sum of the parts—they enhance each other. Sadly, sometimes this special connection, this passion becomes diluted amid the stresses of everyday life. It becomes malnourished, even sick. Maintaining a strong, successful relationship takes constant work, sacrifice, and continuous commitment and recommitment.

The keys to preserving an enduring, healthy bond with your partner are communication, honesty, respect, and commitment. Too often, couples are not willing to go the distance—they are more inclined to want to throw in the towel at the first sign of trouble. It's too much work. If you are experiencing particular problems in your marriage or committed relationship, even infidelity, don't be so quick to let the relationship dissolve without at least attempting to repair and, hopefully, restore the situation. If you feel yourself drifting from your partner, try to remember what brought the two of you together in the first place. Think of the world you have created together. And above all, be open with your partner.

Talk honestly about what you believe is causing you to lose sight of each other. Make it clear that you want to work on your relationship, not allow it to whither and die. Let him or her know you want to recapture and rekindle the romance and excitement that drew you to each other in the first place. Together, try to make a sincere effort at rebuilding your bond before it crumbles. It takes a concerted effort to become sensitive to each other's needs, views, and interests. Focus on the assets you have amassed together, not the negatives. Earlier in this book, you found out that many people have affairs in order to reinvent themselves—to break free of the roles they feel stuck in. Why won't a loving couple do the same?

> *Kathleen learned from her own infidelity not to take her marriage for granted. It took time, but she and her husband, Dave, were able to rebuild their relationship, and now they are closer than ever. At least once a week, Kathleen sweeps through the grocery store tossing a few of their favorite snacks—strawberries and chocolates, some pâté with crispbreads, or brie with grapes and crackers—into her basket along with a bottle of champagne. Later that night, she and Dave will lay out a blanket and have a candlelight picnic somewhere in their house (anywhere but the bedroom). They will feed each other tidbits and get a little silly, enjoying each other as they did when they were newlyweds.*

## EMOTIONAL EQUITY

Together, committed couples build equity in their relationships. This is a treasure trove of shared goals, mutual memories of good times and bad, and joint experiences. This fund of "emotional equity" deserves serious respect; after all, it has taken considerable time to build. Let's not abandon it when times get tough. As your relationship encounters difficulties—and all relationships do—draw from this special fund to give yourselves the strength to keep things going, to keep you from losing sight of one another. Draw on the cherished times you've shared, on the happy memories, and the good times. Reflect back and remember the obstacles you have overcome in the past. Remember some of those past warm feelings and gain strength from them. Keep in mind that as long as your relationship has something left in this "bank," there is hope.

When infidelity hits home, many couples are quick to end their relationships. Betrayed spouses tend to seek legal counsel immediately, often urged on by well-meaning friends and family members. But lawyers are not therapists or marriage counselors. They are not there to handle the turmoil and the wreckage of a marriage. They will not encourage the two of you to "work it out." They have no vested interest in seeing the marriage survive. Before making any drastic moves to end your relationship, I urge you to make an attempt to begin relationship building. This could mean working with a marriage counselor or joining a support group. No one is saying this will be easy, and there are no guarantees that the marriage will survive in spite of your efforts, but at least you'll know you have given it your best. You owe it to yourself and your partner.

## SUMMING IT UP

As seen in Chapter 1, temptation, feeling attracted to others, is common among couples. Even the most happily married, most devout, most conservative people feel an attraction to others. Indulging in daydreams about being with someone other than your partner is not unusual. Such fantasies can feel exciting and pleasurable. Acting on them, however, is where the danger lies and the consequences happen.

If you are contemplating an affair or are already involved in one, discover the driving force behind it. What is propelling the relationship in the first place? What do you think an affair will bring that is missing from your marriage or relationship? Examine what this lover, this affair, would allow you to be. What facet of yourself do you hope to explore within this relationship? Is it for attention, sexual satisfaction, romance, excitement, or simply the need for someone who will listen to and comfort you?

Explore other alternatives to alleviate these voids in your relationship, *before* you take that unfaithful step. I realize now that one of the biggest mistakes of my life was to leave my husband, the father of my child. We had endured one of the most difficult life passages two people can experience through our daughter's death, and it was only natural that renewal and regrowth in our relationship would take time. I didn't allow the time and healing needed to restore the marriage. I brought an intruder into our relationship, a third party. In essence, I ran away.

Above all, consider the consequences of your actions. Remember to focus where affairs end as you work your way back before making a fateful decision to explore the world of infidelity. As you have seen in this book, there are ramifications to affairs. They happen, and they can happen to you!

# 8 Breaking the Chains That Bind

*"Those who realize their folly are not true fools."*

—Chuang Tzu
4th Century BC

Breaking the cycle of infidelity is all about change. It involves your feelings, thoughts, and actions, and it affects just about everyone around you. Yes, it's about doing and seeing things differently, with a new perspective. Change is about taking charge and intervening positively on your own behalf. It's about finding something else to fill the gap that infidelity has filled.

Once you have made the decision to make a change, be prepared—it will be challenging. It requires consistent behavior. Moving to a new home or changing schools, for example, can require enormous effort and a great deal of courage. And even temporary changes like taking the bus to work while your car is being repaired can create tension and stress. Predictably then, breaking free of unfaithful behavior, especially if it means letting go of someone you feel you deeply love, can be one of life's greatest challenges. Keep in mind, however, that the first step in changing the course of your life is often the most terrifying. Once you have finally made the commitment to do things differently and have actually started down that path, you'll find that the emptiness and turmoil will get easier with the passage of time.

For many people, the mere thought of ending an affair, letting go of a lover, is unthinkable. After all, most people are involved in affairs to begin with because they feel they are gaining something from them. (As you saw in Part One, the reasons for affairs are extensive and multifaceted.) Typically, lovers feel as if they are bonded to each other. I know I did. When I was involved in my last affair and my lover and I were apart, I longed for him. My fantasies, and the spirit of the relationship was with me constantly. He never really left my thoughts. This is one of the reasons many people resist breaking free of such behavior. Others may fear that ending the affair may send their lovers into fits of rage, possibly wreaking vengeful havoc all around. (Remember the frighteningly obsessive lover in the movie *Fatal Attraction*?)

The reasons for procrastination when it comes to ending affairs are as countless as the reasons people enter them in the first place. Most excuses, however, are shaped by the same underlying reason—the fear of change. I know when I finally decided to break the bonds of adulterous behavior for good, I can still remember the feelings of panic and terror this decision invoked. Each time I gained the strength to try to end the relationship, I found reasons to keep it going. I was afraid of change. I feared the pain of ending the relationship would be far greater than continuing it. I believed I was deeply in love, and the thought of life without this man appeared to be far more catastrophic than the damaging consequences of the affair itself. On those few occasions when I felt strong enough to leave my lover, he talked me out of it. So the cycle continued. Deep within me I knew I had to break this pattern, but I felt powerless to make it happen. Sound familiar?

Eventually, my renewed spiritual faith enabled me to come to terms with my infidelity in order to break free of its chains. I discovered my real soul mate was within me, and I had, therefore, the strength to face my responsibilities and finally be accountable for my actions.

## CHANGE MEANS RISK

Change can feel frightening because the road ahead winds through unfamiliar territory. But once you have decided to break the bonds of an affair, you have overcome the first obstacle in the road. It's time to stay focused as you forge ahead.

In some ways ending an affair and putting it behind you is like driving down a two-lane highway behind a lumbering truck. You want to pass it, get ahead of it, but there's sporadic oncoming traffic. In order to pass the truck, you have to pick your moment carefully. At one point, you think you can make it but then you see an oncoming car and you maintain your place behind the truck. A few minutes later, you see an opportunity and try again. Moving up alongside the truck, you spot a car coming at you in the distance. But there's no turning back now—you've passed the point of no return. So with the gas pedal to the floor, you speed ahead, determined to get ahead of the truck. There's a moment of panic, of terror, as the oncoming car seems to be racing toward you, but you stay focused and concentrate on your driving. With eyes firmly ahead, you stay focused on your objective, then . . . whoosh . . . you've made it. You passed the truck and navigated your way successfully back into your lane. The road ahead is clear.

Any life change requires a similar series of steps. You must mentally prepare for what you have to do, decide to do it, commit to this decision, then start the process. Once you've started, you may face a challenge or two, but you have to continue forward, staying focused on your objective. The further along you get, the greater the sense of accomplishment you'll achieve. Suddenly, almost without noticing how you got there, you'll realize you're more than halfway to your goal. When you're in the home stretch, you'll feel confident that you can make it. And once you've stopped to catch your breath, a feeling of exhilaration will take over. It may have been very difficult, but it's over and you have made it.

## SET CLEAR OBJECTIVES

Remember, no matter where you are in the life cycle of an affair, there is always the option of letting go. As you strive to bring closure to an affair, consider the following realistic objectives. Resolve to:

- Intervene on your own behalf. Remind yourself that you need time to heal. *"If I am to be of help to others I must be healthy. I will give myself the time and resources necessary to stay healthy in mind, spirit, and body."*

- Gain the courage to ask for what you need and want. Put false pride aside and reach out for the help and support you deserve. *"I will take the steps necessary for my recovery because I am responsible for it. I will gain strength in myself and my choices."*

- Determine to take better care of yourself. Keep an open mind as you become aware of your resources and options. Take advantage of and implement the power that new information, fresh ideas, and forgiveness can bring. *"I am not a victim. I am a valuable person whose needs are important. I can do what is necessary to bring order to my life. I will live in reality and turn my back on my delusions and outlandish fantasies."*

Keep in mind that the first steps are always the most difficult. Also remember that you have the power to take those steps.

## TAKE THAT FIRST STEP

Breaking away from the bonds of infidelity requires a willingness to strip off your mask and move forward sincerely, honestly, and openly. It means laying bare your thoughts and fears so that you can break the cycle. It is a singular act of courage. Taking that first step can be staggeringly painful, but it is necessary. Maybe you are at a point in your affair at which the pain is beginning to outweigh the pleasure—the point at which you begin to unmask your lover and notice the "chinks in the armor." Believe or not, you can live without your lover. I understand the agony of ending an affair, but this hurt won't last forever. On the contrary, the suffering you will feel by staying involved in your affair will last a lot longer. Remember, you entered this relationship of your own free will. Now, exercising that same free will, you can also choose to end it.

Like drinking, gambling, or overeating, infidelity is often characterized by habitual, compulsive behavior. Such destructive patterns often have a lot in common. If you have ever tried to quit smoking or work through another dependency, you know that ending the cycle can be most effective by stopping the destructive behavior abruptly. Breaking any dependency requires the following steps:

1. Acknowledging the behavior.

2. Recognizing the need for change.

3. Becoming ready and willing to change.

4. Becoming accountable.

5. Finding the resources to help change occur.

6. Breaking free of the behavior.

Inevitably, that first step—distancing yourself from your lover—is a most difficult but crucial one, especially in the beginning. As hard as this may be, it's important for you to sever all connections, close the lines of communication, end all contact. This means no phone calls, letters, or e-mails. At the onset, you will undoubtedly find this an arduous task. Receiving positive support from a therapist, a good friend, or even a parent can help you get through this. Bear in mind that ending the relationship is empowering. This empowerment will replace that "something" you were getting from the relationship.

Once the first step has been taken and your course has been set, it's important for you to take it one day at a time. This is an important concept to adopt when experiencing any change. Don't overwhelm yourself with worries about the distant future. When you wake up in the morning, tell yourself that you're going to make it through the day without seeing or talking to your lover, despite the feelings of loneliness and emptiness this may cause. At the end of the day, congratulate yourself and resolve to do it again tomorrow.

Don't dismiss this "one-day-at-a-time" philosophy as an empty slogan. It is a practical, workable method that is used extensively in programs designed to help people overcome their dependencies. It will work for overcoming your relationship as well. It is a deeply spiritual commitment to making your new life count one moment, one step, one day at a time. Some people in early recovery may need to break this down even further—possibly to one hour at a time. Thinking in small increments helps make change manageable and palatable, and it will more likely lead to success. But what happens if you backslide during a moment of weakness? Don't be too hard on yourself. It happens. The important thing is not to let it prevent you from starting again. Persevere. Believe in yourself and your ability to create change and make things happen. For me, what worked best was keeping in mind the wisdom of the following ancient Chinese proverb: the journey of a thousand miles begins with a single step.

## ACCOUNTABILITY

You are currently involved in an affair and you know you should break free of it. You have talked yourself in and out of ending this hurtful behavior a number of times, but you can't seem to take that first step. To help gain the strength you need to take action—to step forward—you must first take responsibility for your behavior and become accountable for your actions. In addition to yourself, consider all of the other people to whom you are accountable. It is owning who you are and your behavior.

## To Yourself

Many people ignore the lessons from past mistakes and continue to push forward impulsively, only to repeat the same mistakes over and over again. I did this from the time I was very young. I tried to escape the pain of my father's death by moving from one troubled relationship to another, never stopping long enough to evaluate my actions. My choices impacted the people around me, subjecting them to hurts and rejections. Ultimately, however, the person who lost the most was me.

Becoming accountable to yourself is a daunting task. It's incredibly difficult to face the mistakes of your past, but in many ways it's not as hard as repeating them over and over again. It takes a great deal of courage and humility to look at one's self. It is a painful process. This is something I learned over time. Unfortunately I learned it the hard way.

In facing my own reality and becoming accountable to myself, one of the most difficult challenges was standing still long enough to look at my life and assess my situation honestly. Only then was I able to begin understanding the choices I'd made and how they had affected my life. Looking back, I saw the damaging pattern I had created—I continually added new baggage before I took the time to unpack the old. When I finally made the decision to stop running, I found that I was actually able to hear the sound of my own heart and mind. Over time, and with the help of an inspiring therapist and the strength of my spiritual faith, I gradually gained the power to own my behavior and face the poor decisions I had made. This enabled me to stop repeating them, to break the chains. Once I had decided to become accountable for my own well-being and finally take charge of my destiny, I felt an incredible relief. It was as if a heavy load had been lifted from my shoulders. And it had.

## To Your Spouse

Accountability to your spouse—the person you once cared enough to marry, regardless of your reasons at the time—begins with respect and commitment. These are the keys to a successful, healthy relationship. They enable you to trust that person with your most intimate secrets; and allow you to appreciate and value his or her feelings, as well. Respect gives you and your partner the strength to work out any problems in your relationship without interference from a third party.

The respect that two committed people have for each other lays the foundation for their emotional "equity"—which builds over time. This fund of good will and shared experiences was what I discarded when I left the father of my child. Instead of borrowing from it to get over the hurdle of my daughter's illness and death, I ran from it. It is this source of strength that you squander when you choose to have an affair, or when you have unprotected sex, or when you neglect your children to be with your lover.

"Till death do us part" was the vow you made when you got married. Too often, these words become meaningless as we turn our backs on our mates when we're bored, find someone more exciting, or simply stop caring. I believe we should think of these words as "lifetime" vows instead of marriage vows.

Accountability to your spouse can begin or resume at any time. Even if you are married and an extramarital affair has entered the picture, realizing your accountability to your spouse can be critical in helping you end the affair and save your marriage. With mutual respect, the pieces can be put back together and the marriage can be strengthened and restored. And let's face it, sometimes the marriage simply is not salvageable. It happens. But if the parties involved respect each other enough, the marriage can end with dignity.

## To Your Children

As discussed in Chapter 6, children are the innocent ones. They suffer the consequences and often bear deep-seated emotional scars as a result of infidelity. Having respect for your children and being accountable to them is probably best displayed through honesty. Be truthful while protecting them from hurtful or extraneous information they don't need to know. They deserve your love and guidance in helping them understand your situation, as well as your obligation as a parent.

## To Your Extended Family, Friends, and Colleagues

In most marriages, the extended family, friends, and even coworkers often play a significant role. Parents, siblings, cousins, uncles, and aunts, as well as best friends, acquaintances, and even people you work with are often involved in many of the ups and downs, the joys and sorrows of a couple's marriage. When these people find themselves on the outskirts of an affair, they usually react by trying to help in some way.

An extramarital affair can seriously destroy close-knit relationships that once existed between these people. Healthy relationships between cheating spouses and their in-laws, for example, can be ruined. Friendships are strained and working relationships are burdened. Constant dependence on friends for support (as well as a source of alibis) can place an unnecessary burden on them. Bringing an affair into the workplace can place added strain on relationships with colleagues. Accountability to these people means considering others rather than the self-centeredness of the affair, and realizing the stress under which you have placed them. It means respecting their boundaries, knowing that it is unfair to place them in compromising situations.

## A LITTLE HELP, PLEASE

Terminating a love affair is one of life's most troublesome undertakings. Putting a permanent end to such behavior can be overwhelming. And trying to get through such difficult times alone can seem like a superhuman feat. Don't be afraid or ashamed to admit you need help, which is a sign of maturity and wisdom. You may find the support you need from a good friend, family member, or someone from the clergy. Professional counseling is another recommended avenue. Recording your thoughts is also a powerful activity for helping you achieve your goals. (See journal writing on page 126.)

### Insight Through Therapy

Professional support through therapy is one of the most beneficial ways to gain an impartial, clear-sighted viewpoint to aid you through trying times. The guidance of a qualified, insightful therapist or participation in a support group can provide just the right outlet for healing and recovery. It will help you better cope with and work through the unsettling emotions you may have as the result of your behavior. Counseling also helps put anger and blame (either toward yourself or others) into proper perspective. During my own recovery process, I found that therapy improved my mental and physical health.

If you have decided to seek professional help, you may not know where to begin. Therapists come if various guises. A *psychiatrist* is a physician who has done a residency in psychiatry. He or she is authorized to prescribe medication in addition to providing psychotherapy sessions. A *clinical psychologist* is trained and educated to perform psychological research and testing. He or she is also trained in group dynamics and individual motivation. There are also *counselors* and *therapists* with degrees in social work, and therapists trained in psychodynamic (Freudian) theory and various other forms of alternative and holistic therapies. Depending on your needs, pick the professional who is best suited for you. Choose someone who specializes in problems similar to yours.

As with any professional, one way to find a therapist is through referrals. Your family doctor or a close friend or family member may be a reliable source. Or contact professional organizations such as the American Medical Association or the Mental Health Association for referrals.

Before committing yourself to a specific therapist, schedule a "get-acquainted" session. It's important for you to feel comfortable—to "click" with—this individual with whom you will be sharing confidential information. This is a very important relationship, one that can make the difference in your healing and recovery process. Take your time. Be prepared before meeting with a therapist for the first time. Jot down any questions or concerns you may want to discuss before committing to starting therapy sessions. The following questions can act as a foundation:

- What are your credentials?

- How long have you been practicing?

- Do you specialize in working with a particular type of person? (adults, children, groups, homosexuals, same-sex couples, etc.)

- What do you consider your role?

- What can I expect from working with you?

- What do you expect from me?

- Approximately how many sessions do you anticipate I will need?

- What is your fee?

If the caregiver is unwilling to answer your questions or seems uncomfortable when you ask them, consider going elsewhere. But don't give up. Look for someone who is well-versed and experienced in dealing with issues surrounding couples and infidelity. If you have strong religious beliefs, be sure to mention it and ask how he or she feels about this. It is in your best interest to work with someone who respects and understands your religious beliefs as well as your particular circumstance.

Some may find individual counseling most effective for their needs. Others may feel sessions with their partners to be best. And in still other instances, group sessions involving all three parties can be the best route.

### Join a Support Group

In addition to therapy sessions, many people find participation in support groups to be helpful. Being able to talk to and share your stories and concerns with others who have had similar experiences can be a source of often-needed strength.

One of the major problems with support groups of this nature, however, is that so few of them exist. You can easily find organizations to help deal with many negative behaviors—drug and alcohol abuse, gambling, shoplifting, overeating, and even sex addiction, to name just a few. However, when it comes to dealing with infidelity, support groups are few and far between. To locate such a group in your area, or to learn how to start your own, contact:

*Face Reality, Inc.*
*PO Box 8593*
*Cincinnati, OH 45208–0593*
*1-800-5AFFAIR*
*www.facereality.com*

### Keep a Journal

"The discipline of the written word," said John Steinbeck, "punishes both stupidity and dishonesty." I believe that one of the most useful, life-enhancing, strengthening steps you can take as you struggle to break from the clutches of infidelity is to keep a journal. It doesn't matter in which stage of the journey you are—at the onset and fearful of the bumpy road ahead, in the middle of the maelstrom and reeling from the changes, or at the end of the process and looking back at how far you have come—jotting down your thoughts, experiences, feelings, and insights can help you focus on yourself, your objectives, and your future. A comforting note is that you don't have to write like a Steinbeck to keep a journal. What you do need is a sincere willingness to write honestly about how you feel. The events of your life, as well as the accompanying feelings and emotions, can be overwhelming. As you write in your journal, you'll discover a clear picture of where you have been, where you are now, and where you're headed. It's an invaluable compass on your journey of self-discovery.

It was only after years of going in and out of affairs, marriages, and relationships that I made the decision to keep daily entries of my experiences. My reasons for starting a journal probably had more to do with validation than anything else: I wanted a place where I could justify myself and what I did and thought. At the onset, I didn't really think that writing these feelings would help me understand or even change the way I handled various situations. I saw it mainly as an effective way to vent my frustrations and anger and immortalize the joyful and memorable events in my life. By writing them down, I was also able to commit to and refer to them later on, which turned out to be both a comfort as well as a source of shame.

In *Infidelity, A Survival Guide,* author Don-David Lesterman says a journal is a private place where you can document your feelings, fears, hopes, and setbacks. It's a place to be yourself, totally and with no holds barred. It allows you the space and the freedom to write out your fantasies and dreams, your disappointments and your hurts. Over time, through the entries I had written, I began to recognize patterns, which gave me the insight I needed to change. Only then was I able to face my fears and choose the direction I wanted to go, with wisdom rather through blind impulse.

Writing became a way of life for me. It can be for you, too. In addition to being private and anonymous, writing:

- Can be done in secrecy and its confidentiality respected.

- Allows you to be totally honest. There's no need to be concerned with how you look to others or how they might be affected by what you say as you bare your soul on paper.

- Can begin immediately, without any help or involvement from anyone else.

- Allows you to engage in daily conversations with yourself, enabling you to express and reveal your innermost thoughts and feelings.

- Helps curb the need to repeat certain thoughts and feeling to anyone else.

- Enables you to vent your anger, keeping personal confrontations to a minimum. Diffusing pent-up emotions helps avoid violent outbursts and conflicts.

- Helps you think through your responses and consider what you should do before you do it. It's a means of evaluating your motives and strategies *before* you act. This is especially helpful if you tend to be impulsive.

- Causes you to understand other people's viewpoints, as you put yourself in their shoes.

Make a commitment to write every day and read your entries often. Think about what you've written. This will help you avoid making the same mistakes over again. You'll begin to see how your attitudes, feelings, and ways of responding change over time.

## RECLAIM YOURSELF

Once you have reset the direction of your behavior, it is important to stay active. Isolating yourself and being idle can cause you to dwell on your situation, which can easily lead you back to old behaviors. Instead, try to fill the void once occupied by your affair with positive substitutes. Engage in activities you enjoy. If you have children, spend more time with them. Pursue hobbies or sports you like. Take up something you always wanted to but never had the time for. Maybe enroll in a class or begin a course of study that interests you—colleges and universities welcome people of all ages. Do some volunteer work, join a club, or redecorate that spare room you've been putting off. Do just about anything that brings you satisfaction and fulfillment (other than having another affair or acquiring another addiction).

As you begin to reclaim yourself, you'll gain the strength and self-esteem necessary to go forward. You will be able to let go of whatever has been dragging you down. This could be your lover as well as your spouse. Or it could be an idealized view of what "could" be rather than what is. Perhaps it is an unresolved grief, or feelings of unworthiness. It might be an unfulfilling job or an unhealthy environment in which you cannot thrive. Whatever it is, start with an honest assessment and hold steadfast in your resolve to change.

When you begin to let go of the situations that are causing your suffering, you have begun the healing process. This process isn't about shame and guilt. It's about self-examination and self-discovery, learning to live in harmony with a changed viewpoint, one that recognizes outcomes before you make the choices that can bring them about. It's about living a life that's in balance and reaching out to people you love as you nurture the inner you. It's about hope and the faith to succeed.

## SUMMING IT UP

Before deciding on a course of action in your fight for fidelity, first it's important to evaluate your own particular situation. Each person, each story, each affair is similar. You are the only one who can determine the reasons you went down the road

129

you did; you're also the one who needs to find your way onto another, more positive road. It is your life, your destiny, your choice. You are the only one who can value yourself enough to make such a change.

# 9 The Courage to Heal

*"Sit openly . . . to the weather as to grief.*
*Or do you think you can shut grief in?"*

—William Carlos Williams

Whether it's the termination of a marriage after many years or the end of a six-month affair, "breaking up," to quote the song, "is hard to do." And it doesn't matter what stage of dissolution the partnership is in—the beginning of a breakup, the middle of a trial separation, or the aftermath of a divorce—any shake-up in the status of a relationship between two people involves grief.

Our society tends to minimize this issue as a sign of weakness. The people we are taught to admire are those who are stoic and strong—those who don't show signs of hurting. And grief is tolerated even less for those involved in adultery. Nobody cares to console the man or woman who is suffering in some way as the result of an affair. Few people feel compassion for the man whose wife has left him after discovering his involvement with another woman. They are more apt to blame him for causing his own problems. The woman whose lover has left her to pursue someone else shouldn't expect much sympathy from those around her—after all, most people will believe that it serves her right. But the reality is that these people are truly hurting. The pain and loss they feel is very real and can be as great as that which is felt by the person whose spouse dies suddenly. They often feel alone, hidden in the shadows and isolated in their grief, forced to keep their pain and suffering inside.

It's no wonder that emotionally we are ill-equipped to cope with loss. Authors John W. James and Frank Cherry point out in *The Grief Recovery Workbook* (New York: Harper and Row, 1988) that we are often raised on myths about grieving that do not promote recovery. How often have you heard the following?

- **It is better to deny or bury true feelings than it is to express them.** When dealing with a loss of any kind—a job, a pet, a friendship, a scholarship, etc.—have you ever been told to "shake it off" and not feel bad? This is an encouragement to discount your authentic responses, your true feelings.

- **You can replace the loss.** Even though this is clearly impossible, it is something we are taught to believe. For example, a child who has just lost a pet may be told, "That's all right. We'll get you another." (In some cases, however, such a replacement *can* serve as a helpful substitute.)

- **You need to grieve alone.** Society, uncomfortable with loss, does not prepare us to comfort others or to gain comfort from others.

In addition to what we are taught from such common myths, loss causes many people to regret the past, wishing things could have been "better, different, more." Afraid to move forward, many individuals hold onto memories and enshrine times gone by. Others strive to insulate themselves from any future pain and suffering by closing themselves off to new relationships, new opportunities.

## GRIEF

Grieving is painful no matter who you are or what your circumstance. But it is also a necessary and significant process for anyone who is faced with a significant loss. Failure to grieve can manifest itself, sometimes many years later, in internalized stress. This can lead to physical and psychological problems, ranging from headaches and stomach upset to panic attacks and more serious medical conditions such as heart problems. Unresolved grief impedes a person's capacity to move forward. In the aftermath of an affair and the wounds they have caused, people can suffer from years of sadness, bitterness, false hopes, guilt, shame, anger, and even severe depression.

The end of any relationship, whether it is the result of a death, divorce, or breakup, involves much more than simply grieving for a lost partner. Grief stretches out in many directions. People grieve for the loss of their own identity as it was defined within the relationship. They may grieve for what they had in the past, for what they now lack in the present, and for what might have been in the future. People are expected to adjust to the loss of the world they had built with their partners, as well as the future they had planned. Betrayal generates loss, whether it is the loss of marital loyalty, dreams, self-esteem, trust, honesty, respect, or a shared future. It is also a great generator of tangible losses such as homes, children, finances, careers, spouses, and lovers. The result is usually a deluge of emotions, sorrow being the most prominent.

*Sue is a slight, slim woman in her mid-thirties who's been married for six years. Her husband Hank, a plastic surgeon, is a busy outgoing man much admired and respected by his patients and colleagues. They have two children, a lovely home, and what appears to be the perfect life. When Sue found out that Hank had been having an affair with his nurse for the last three years, she couldn't believe it. It had to be a mistake. But Hank confessed that it was true. He just needed the excitement, the "extra" of an affair. He claimed that he still loved Sue and their children, minimizing the affair as just a "hobby." He begged Sue to forgive him.*

*Angry and brokenhearted, Sue considered leaving Hank, but she didn't want to break up her family and the life they had together. She told Hank she would stay with him as long as he stopped seeing his lover. He promised he would, and they agreed not to talk about it anymore. But as time went on, Sue realized that she just couldn't forget about it. She lost her appetite and began losing weight. Her once perfectly proportioned body began to appear frail, her face became drawn. She found herself crying for no reason at the strangest times—when peeling potatoes for dinner or after dropping off the kids at nursery school. Her grief, which she kept bottled up inside, was so intense that there were times when she thought she was going mad.*

One thing is certain, affairs cause grief in some degree or another. It can be felt by some or all of those involved in or touched by an affair—the betrayed husband, the jilted lover, the philandering wife, or the child caught up in a parent's affair. Grief is a complex emotion, characterized by deep mental anguish and intense sorrow. Individuals differ in how they are able to express their grief and the time they need to recuperate from it. There isn't a specific set of rules that applies to everyone. Emotions swing wildly from one extreme to another as those involved adjust to their physical, financial, social, parental, and spiritual changes. And grief takes time and effort to work through.

If you are in the throes of a breakup, you may find that you can't sleep or eat, or that there is a constant lump in your throat or aching pain in your heart. You may feel confused and disoriented, or nervous and irritable much of the time. During this time, remember to consider just how fragile you are and focus on those positive steps to help yourself. Try not to keep your feelings bottled inside. Talk to someone you feel you can trust—a therapist, person of the clergy, close friend, or family member. You need someone who is objective who will listen as you air your feelings. During this time of emotional upheaval, it is not wise to make any major life decisions. Defer such moves until you are stronger and more emotionally grounded.

## THE STAGES OF GRIEF

Each person has his or her individual way of coping with grief—there is no right or wrong way. Some people opt for privacy and solitude, while others are more vocal in their mourning. According to Dr. Elizabeth Kübler-Ross, author of *On Death and Dying* (New York: MacMillan Publishing, 1969), there are five stages of the grieving process—denial, anger, bargaining, depression, and acceptance—that you can expect to go through when dealing with death or any other significant loss.

## Denial

"This can't be happening." This first, almost instinctual response to loss buys us a little time because it helps keep us numb, at least to some extent. During this stage, we can also feel intense pain, euphoria, confusion, or all of the above. This is the point at which the loss has us reeling with shock. Different people feel various things during the denial stage. Some may feel a terrible sense of self-hatred or rejection, while others may have moments of relief and happiness with their newfound freedom. Some individuals become very restless, nervous, and irritable; others become reclusive and silent.

I denied my grief for most of my life. The loss of my father when I was still a teenager set this stage for denial. Later, I found myself hopelessly stuck in denial again as I lost my only child to leukemia, and then later on as I lost my stepdaughter to infidelity. I denied my pain and suffering—continuously running from it instead of facing it. I made many poor decisions in a futile attempt to come to grips with my grief and the work necessary to come to terms with my losses. And the process does involve work. It hurts, it's time-consuming, and it's heart-wrenching. I didn't want to face that heartbreak, so I ran from it, always turning to new people, new relationships, and new interests to mask my sorrow. My actions resulted in, among other things, a succession of failed marriages and extramarital affairs. Years later, when I finally stopped running, my grief, like an unyielding sentry, was still there, waiting for me.

## Anger

After the initial reaction to a loss, anger is often the next emotion to surface, and it is usually targeted in many directions—at spouses or lovers, at God, at the hand fate has dealt, at the unfairness of it all. Anger can also be self-directed as we become furious with ourselves for our destructive actions. We may berate ourselves for being so impulsive, so blind, or for having made so many poor choices.

As for those who have been unwillingly betrayed by their unfaithful partners, anger is certainly understandable. They entered into their relationships (whether marriages, committed monogamous partnerships, or even love affairs) in good faith, expecting exclusivity, loyalty, and commitment. Instead they are left with feelings of hurt and rejection.

## Bargaining

In a desperate attempt to salvage their relationships, people often turn to God or a higher power to strike a bargain. "If this works out, I promise to become more involved in my child's interests" . . . "I'll do volunteer work at the local hospital" . . . "I'll never cheat on my partner again" . . . and on and on. Making desperate deals may help us cope with our emotions for a time, but as the grief process continues, so does the realization that such deals simply don't work.

As the thought of separation mounts, many people attempt to salvage their relationships by bargaining with their partners. There may be promises to reform philandering ways, to quit drinking, to stop watching so much football or playing bridge. Occasionally, such "deals" may lead to reconciliation; however, in most cases, the reunions are temporary and merely delay the inevitable. Often during this period of uneasy reconciliation comes the realization that the relationship really is over.

## Depression

"I had no idea I could hurt so much and endure such suffering." Depression is the most consuming and difficult stage of grief to navigate. As the full impact of loss sinks in, so does sorrow, and almost at a primal level. It is often characterized by feelings of hopelessness, lack of control, and defeat. Emotions such as guilt, hurt, shame, and fear often accompany depression. Some people wallow in this state, preoccupied with thoughts of what went wrong and why. Others become confused, bitter, and resentful.

Depression can be frightening and polarizing. Many people I have encountered in support groups have expressed feeling "locked in their suffering," wondering if they will ever come out of it. Others worry that they might be having a breakdown of some sort. Sometimes these feelings of sadness and grief can be so overwhelming, there's a temptation to bury them. "I am afraid that if I start to cry I'll never stop" is a common fear, but tears can be a positive vehicle for easing uncomfortable emotions. Opening up to emotions is one of the safest ways to cleanse the soul and help bring closure to grief.

Although depression can be paralyzing, actually it can be a protective, healthy response to loss. It slows you down and gives you a chance to regroup, rethink. It is a time for insight and self-discovery. "Falling apart" can be viewed as a promising sign that things can be put back together again. It is helpful to think of this period as a time of creative introspection, a time in which internal energies should be directed towards increased self-awareness and a new start. Depression can be that transitional stage that helps us reorder our lives.

Remember, it is important to allow yourself time to acknowledge your real (although uncomfortable) feelings and experience them fully, but don't stay stuck in your misery for so long that you are unwilling to let go of the suffering after a reasonable amount of time. You will only further injure yourself. Don't allow yourself to sink so low into the quagmire of your emotions that you forget to come up for air. It will smother your sense of well-being. Keep in mind that what has happened, for whatever reason, has happened. It's over. You cannot change the past; you need to connect with it as you intervene on your own behalf. Allow compassion and forgiveness for yourself and others. These are healing in and of themselves, and will help you make progress in your recovery. During this time, talking to someone you trust or jotting down your thoughts and feelings can be especially helpful in keeping you focused and on track.

## Acceptance

As time passes and feelings of grief begin to subside, most people find that somehow they have worked through the chaos of their situation, and their lives have settled into some semblance of order. They have come to terms with the loss, and have found the strength and courage to keep going on. This form of acceptance heralds the final stage of the grieving process. It is about accepting the fact that certain things cannot be changed or reversed. It allows us to move somewhat beyond the grief and into a stage in which closure is only a step away.

Hanging onto bitterness, sadness, and anger for too long, no matter how devastating the breakup, is counter-productive for everyone, especially children. Through this stage, we empower ourselves to become more self-reliant, stronger. We are better equipped to make sound decisions about children, finances, careers, and living arrangements. The loss, which once occupied all of our attention, begins to fade, permitting us to deal with other issues. Fear, guilt, shame, and other emotions we faced during the grieving period begin to recede, allowing us to reconstruct our sense of self—who we are and how we fit into the world. No longer are we weighed down with sorrow. Each day brings renewed energy and we have the capacity to feel more positive. We can allow ourselves to feel hopeful about a future that now seems more promising.

This is a time to take baby steps into new activities and relationships. It is also vitally important to remember that lapsing back into an earlier stage of anger or depression is common and a natural part of the grieving process. If you find yourself sliding back into a sea of negative emotions, consider opening up your journal and writing a goodbye letter to your former partner and the life you once had. This will help you say what you may not have said before and allow you to experience a final mourning period for the ending of a relationship you expected would last your lifetime. The road to recovery relinquishes the past. It means letting go as you move forward in a new direction.

## THE POWER OF FORGIVENESS

*Ellen has fantasies of blowing up the car of her ex-husband, Phil. She also considers writing a letter to his boss, describing all of the terrible things Phil ever said about him. She lies awake nights hoping he'll contract a horrible illness. She wishes that Cathy, his new and very young girlfriend, will dump Phil and hurt him as badly as he hurt her.*

*Ellen's anger is understandable. Not only had Phil left her for another woman, he had taken a substantial amount of money from their joint savings account to use as a down payment on a condo, which he shared with his new love.*

*At first, she refused to believe the rumor. Hadn't they just spent a wonderful weekend at that romantic bed and breakfast in Maine? But once the truth came out and Phil told Ellen he wanted out of their marriage so he could move in with Cathy, her disbelief quickly turned to anger—a bitter and all-consuming fury. She became obsessed with the desire to hurt him—hurt them both. For months it was all she could talk about to her friends and family, who seemed to understand and staunchly support her. Eventually, however, although they sympathized with Ellen, they began to tire of her vengeful obsession. Ellen knew her anger was destructive, and she also realized she was alienating herself from family and friends.*

*Ellen continued hating Phil passionately with every ounce of her being, but soon this anger began to wear her down. She became tired both mentally and physically. Suddenly, Ellen felt her anger transform into a kind of melancholy, and she began obsessing over the life she and Phil once had together. Always exhausted, she dragged herself through each day and spent many nights alone, staring blankly at her television set with a box of tissues to wipe her tears and a bottle of wine to dull her pain—a deep-seated sadness. Mornings became increasingly difficult for Ellen to get out of bed, and she began calling in sick for work more and more often. She also stopped going out to lunch on Fridays with her friends—a tradition that had begun during their college days—and she began politely excusing herself from attending family functions.*

*Ellen's mom and sister tried their best to support Ellen and help pull her out of the downward spiral she was in; but they were fruitless in their attempts. It became clear to them that Ellen needed professional help. With their encouragement, Ellen began seeing a therapist, who helped her work through the grief and pain. Eventually, she was able to face her uncomfortable emotions honestly, validate her feelings, and then eventually let them go. In essence, she was able to admit and accept her loss. Only then was she able to move forward.*

*Many months later, when Ellen heard that Phil and*

*Cathy were getting married, she actually sent them a card, wishing them well. Most of Ellen's friends couldn't believe it. They felt she was letting Phil off the hook.*

In reality, Ellen did not let Phil off the hook. She let herself off the hook. After months of sleepless nights fraught with anger, bitterness, and deep-rooted sadness, Ellen realized that by forgiving Phil, she was able to move on with her own life. With the support of her mom, sister, and a few good friends, and through talks with her therapist, who encouraged her to write down her feelings, Ellen took control of her life. She chose to make a peaceful closure instead of waging war over what had happened and gave herself permission to live a more harmonious life. She realized the damage caused by hanging onto her hurt and anger far outweighed the benefits she could gain by forgiving Phil.

Ellen understood that forgiveness isn't about condoning the actions of others or even forgetting about them. Rather, it is about creating a change of heart in the way you think, feel, and respond. For as long as she was obsessed with revenge and rage, Ellen was the one who suffered. But by recognizing and accepting her feelings, she was able to overcome the ones that stood in the way of forgiveness. Revenge, anger, and wallowing in sorrow or guilt require enormous amounts of negative energy that do nothing more than sap one's strength. They interfere with healing and hope. When we honestly forgive, we relinquish the need to return hurt for hurt.

Additionally, forgiveness does not necessarily involve reconciling with the person who has hurt you. What it *does* involve is rebuilding the relationship you have with yourself and becoming the person you want to be. It's all about choice—choosing to let go of the anger and resentment that has been weighing you down. It is an act that requires courage and strength of character. It allows the power of the hurt to be diffused. And once you have chosen to forgive, you can teach your heart to love and trust once more. Mark Twain put it beautifully when he said, "Forgiveness is the fragrance that the violet sheds on the heel that stepped on it."

Forgiveness means recognizing that anyone can be dragged down by their own weakness. It is a realization that we are frail, that we are human, that we make mistakes. Being able to forgive is a sign of maturity and strength. It is a positive, life-enhancing choice that initiates healing and fosters closure. It's taking the high road.

## SUMMING IT UP

Infidelity, like any other life-shattering event, inevitably leads to a plethora of emotions. Many choose to deny the situation and run from their pain, never choosing to deal with it. Others drown in their suffering and anger, and they can't seem to leave the past behind them. They are trapped in their distress and relive it every day.

Still others move past the pain of infidelity. They embrace their grief, confront it, then learn how to forgive. It is only after facing the past and the anguish it entails, and being open to forgiveness that a person can truly move on. *Forgiveness is a priceless gift—given to you by you.*

# A Final Word

I have lived through and, thankfully, recovered from the various roles I have played in the love triangles of my life. During these journeys, my heart was shattered and turned upside down, but eventually made whole again. What is done is done. I cannot change any of the decisions of my past. No one can. My hope, however, is that through this book—through my experiences and the experiences of many others—you will gain greater insight and awareness into the world of infidelity. No matter where you are in your life today, I hope this book helps you muster the strength and courage needed to set straight a course that may have gone awry.

An eye-opener into the world of betrayal, this book encourages awareness, prevention, positive intervention, and recovery from this destroyer of hopes, dreams, and lives. Finally, it's about making choices and being accountable for them. And any choice, ultimately, is yours.

# Index